Breakthrough
Medical
Discovery
REVEALS...

Your
Blood
DOESN'T
LIE!

Aging, Disease and Illnesses
Are Linked to
ONE CAUSE...
and ONE SOLUTION!

Sergey A. Dzugan, MD, PhD

George W. Rozakis, MD

with Deborah Mitchell

"UNLOCK YOUR BODY'S NATURAL HEALING ABILITY"

The Dzugan Principle:
Your Blood Doesn't Lie!

ISBN: 978-0-615-33418-9

Printed in the United States of America

***Dedicated to**
the loving and eternal memory of
Alexander "Sasha" Dzugan
whom inspired the work within this book.*

Foreward

....

Richard D. Sutton
Chairman, Royal Resorts Group

Harolyn C. Gilles, M.D.
Bio-identical Hormone Physician

James Hayes, M.D., FAAFP, BCEM
Emergency Room Physician

....

Richard D. Sutton, Chairman
The Royal Resorts Group

I believe this extraordinary book can help you live a long, healthy life. Although I have lived more than three quarters of a century, I am disease-free, take no prescription drugs and my physical age is about twenty years younger than my biological age. And none of this is by accident.

My story begins in 1978 when I moved my family to Cancun, Mexico, after retiring from the US Air Force. There I and my partners developed the Royal Resorts, and in the process of managing food selection, I also became aware of the importance of good nutrition and supplementation. Over the next twenty years I investigated new products. Eventually, however, I experienced a decline in energy, unwanted weight gain and sleep problems. That's when someone introduced me to Dr. Sergey Dzugan. After a battery of blood tests, I immediately began his program of bioidentical hormone therapy along with modifications to my supplementation program.

Seven years later, I am still enthusiastically following the program. My energy level and stamina greatly exceed that of many of my younger colleagues. I am certain that without Dr. Dzugan's guidance in restoring my natural hormonal balance to youthful levels and a specific supplement program, I would not enjoy my superior level of health today.

Harolyn C. Gilles
Bio-identical Hormone Physician

When I first had the privilege of meeting one of Medicine's international all-time greats, Dr. Sergey Dzugan, my first reaction was, "How young and vital this man looks!" I actually could not imagine how he could have amassed 30 years of experience with no evidence of the toll time usually takes on us all. Here stood a man who obviously practices what he preaches. I immediately decided to take heed to whatever he had to teach me. To paraphrase an old adage: "when the student arrives, the teacher will appear". I had arrived!

In the past decade of training under some of leaders in the field of "Anti-Aging Medicine," both here and abroad, I finally had the opportunity to learn from The Best how to put the principles espoused in this book into action to help people look, feel and function optimally. While a poet may have coined the phrase, "Youth is wasted on the young," who says that vim and vigor have to be saved only for the young? In reading this insightful and well-written expose on what exactly to look for, and what can be done in each individual circumstance, you will delight in discovering that first of all, you don't have to look or feel your age, or just learn to "live with it" because it's normal for age. In my opinion, "normal aging" is an OPTION!

I like to refer to what we do as "Pro-active Aging", rather than "Anti-Aging", because of course, no doctor is anti-aging. After all, what's the alternative? In the pages of this power-packed, information-filled book, you will not only learn how and what makes your body age, but most importantly, how, and with the help of Dr. Dzugan and his colleagues all over the world, you can halt, reverse and actually prevent the ravages of the degenerative process known as aging.

Furthermore, the age-old model (no pun intended) of treating diseases with antiquated and potentially harmful medications (which often cause more side effects than benefits), is now being replaced by the Dzugan Principle, which offers remedies such as natural supplements and bioidentical hormones, (which have been proven safe and effective).

Dr. Dzugan has been successful in preventing a myriad of diseases, such as migraines, hypothyroidism, diabetes, high cholesterol, fibromyalgia, erectile dysfunction, menopause and a host of others, which have remained enigmatic to so many personal physicians and specialists alike. In addition, through his well-studied and documented principle, his indisputable methods offer treatments and cures, which restore total health and wellbeing at any age, as well as youthfulness and quality of life for a lifetime. In the words of Dr. Dzugan himself, "It's the results that matter!"

> *Enjoy reading and discovering how you can be all that you were meant to be!*
>
> *Enjoy living life to its fullest!*
>
> *Enjoy the life-changing results the Dzugan Principle has to offer you!*

With the deepest respect, admiration and appreciation,

Proudly, Your colleague and friend,

Harolyn C. Gilles, M.D.
Phoenix, Arizona

Finally, a physiologic and common sense approach to treating the most difficult of patients, including migraine, menopausal, chronic fatigue, depression, fibromyalgia, etc...

Instead of just treating symptoms, Dr's Dzugan and Rozakis provide a complete program that optimizes one's physiology and naturally unlocks the body's healing abilities. They succinctly explain that most conditions have one cause and therefore, similar treatment.

I highly recommend lay and medical practitioners read this book and implement the Dzugan Principle in their practice.

James Hayes, M.D.
FAAFP BCEM
Florida

Table of Contents

Part II: Diseases and Medical Conditions
page 83

Introduction

As tens of millions of baby boomers advance toward their golden years, there is a great deal of interest in medical science and strategies to remain youthful and free of disease.

In the following pages, we introduce you to a brave new world in healing. In Part I, you will learn about our Restorative Medicine Program. Detailed scientific information on the basic elements of our Program, involving the strategic use of bioidentical hormones, nutrients, vitamins and supplements will be presented, and we will review why conventional medicine therapy often does not work, and can in fact cause harm. To the physician reader of this book, we will show you a new paradigm of healing, and we stand ready to assist your entry into this exciting new world of care.

Then in Part II, we explore in detail many of the conditions that respond to hormone restoration treatment -- conditions such as heart disease, high cholesterol, migraine, menopause, gastrointestinal disorders, erectile dysfunction, rheumatoid conditions, cancer, macular degeneration, and psychological disorders. You may wonder how and why hormone restoration can effectively address all of these seemingly diverse health issues. Well, you will soon find out! The use of hormones as therapy is an expanding and fascinating field which at times has been maligned by those forces that stand to lose from its success. In the book we will show that bioidentical hormones are safe and highly effective. We will provide the reader a logical and common sense way of thinking about restorative medicine.

In the past, the public was ill advised in regard to the field of hormones, and we must set this record straight. It may shock the reader to know that **we have never seen a negative report on the proper use of bio-identical hormones!** Many of those studies that you may have heard of used synthetic hormone **drugs**, rather than natural, bio-identical hormones – and those did cause side effects such as breast cancer, clotting disturbances and stroke. **Natural, bio-identical hormones** do not. There is ample literature to condemn the belief that these imposter drugs were identical to natural hormones, yet this misinformation continues to this day. It is impervative that everyone understands the subject, and spread the truth, in the interest of our common health and vitality.

The other confusion that must be dispelled immediately is all the misguided research that has looked at the use of single hormones and single vitamins. This is wrong because our body chemistry is a symphony. Hormones and vitamins and nutrients all interact with each other and various systems in the body. We, therefore, introduce the concept of hormonal balance. Fortunately, we and other innovative clinicians understand the value of looking at the entire hormone picture, and of achieving and maintaining balanced hormone levels in the body.

Another notable fact is that the hormones used in most of the research conducted by mainstream investigators are not chemically identical—commonly referred to as bioidentical--to those produced in humans. In our Restorative Medicine Program, we exclusively use hormones that are bioidentical to human hormones, including pregnenolone, DHEA, estrogens, progesterone, testosterone, cortisol, thyroid hormones and melatonin. Again, we have found that unless people take hormone supplements that are biochemically identical to those produced by the body, the results can be inconsequential at best and damaging at worst. Fortunately, forward-thinking clinicians are increasingly using bioidentical hormones prescribing them to their patients.

The use of hormones that are bioidentical to those manufactured by the human body are the cornerstone of our Restorative Medicine Program explored in this book. Along with hormones, we also recommend nutritional and herbal supplements from natural sources (as needed) to round out each patient's individual treatment program.

We hope you will see how restoring hormonal balance may be the answer you and your loved ones have been looking for when it comes to finding effective, lasting treatment for some of life's most common and disruptive health concerns. We share with you the stories and treatment plans of some of the many participants in this Program, and how they have come to find good health in balance.

We wish the same for you.

Part I

A Revolutionary Approach To

Medicine and Healing

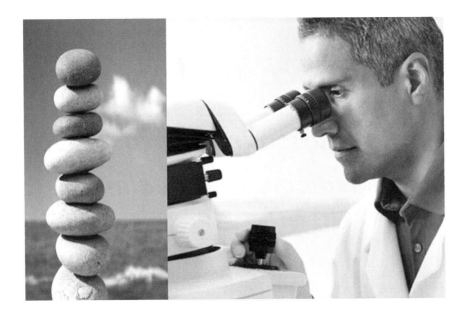

Chapter
1

RESTORATIVE MEDICINE:
A BRAVE NEW WORLD IN HEALING

More than 100 years ago, John Harvey Kellogg, MD—yes, the Kellogg of Battle Creek and cereal fame—said this about Physiologic Medicine: "[it] does not undertake to cure disease, but patients. It recognizes the disease process as an effort on the part of the body to recover normal conditions—a struggle on the part of the vital forces to maintain life under abnormal conditions and to restore vital equilibrium."

In today's words, we would say that the vital force that Dr. Kellogg references is our innate body chemistry or physiology. Disease is the derangement of physiology, from imbalances or deficiencies in our hormones and body chemistry. The body tries to fight these problems using any and all tricks and strategies given to it by Mother Nature, but eventually the body succumbs to the imbalance in the form of diseases we all know, including high cholesterol, migraine, menopause, erectile dysfunction and many more...

Physiologic Medicine is the field of identifying and correcting these abnormalities of physiology, so that the body does not need to struggle in a state of abnormality. When we optimize physiology, we unleash the innate power of the body to fix itself, and fix itself it does. It is as if we untie and unleash our most powerful soldiers who can again begin the process of defending our health. That is the vital force of which Dr. Kellogg speaks.

Today, a century later, the virtues and impressive healing powers of Physiologic Medicine are coming to the fore. A new century—indeed, a new millennium—requires that we give this method an updated, more appropriate name, one that states what it is: **Restorative Medicine** or, more precisely, Hormone-Restorative Medicine.

What is restorative medicine? It is the restoration of optimal physiology. It is a whole-body concept because it affects every organ system, from our head to our toes. Restorative Medicine logically forces **a new principle: that many diseases are the result of an imbalance of body chemistry, and once we restore balance and physiology we can correct the cause of the majority of diseases.** This is the new message that must be heard, and will be heard because it is logical, it is rooted in science, and it is based on clinical results.

The concepts of Restorative Medicine in this book are based on the lifetime work of Sergey A. Dzugan, MD, PhD, who has fine tuned this concept and identified specific essential hormones and nutrients that need to be brought back into equilibrium or balanced to achieve optimal health, and a body able to fight disease. Using our Restorative Medicine Program, clinicians and patients can enter a brave new world in healing and will be able to effectively prevent or treat diseases and syndromes that result from imbalances, such as atherosclerosis, arthritis, migraine, fibromyalgia, menopause, depression, erectile dysfunction, and many others.

What Causes Disease?

To better understand what Restorative Medicine is all about, let's first consider some basic concepts. One is, What causes disease? Once you know what causes a disease or disorder, you have a more solid foundation upon which to find ways to prevent and treat it. Disease can be caused by one of four factors:

- Genetics/Congenital: Conditions such as cystic fibrosis, hemophilia, Down's syndrome, congenital heart disease, and sickle cell have clear genetic or congenital causes. In addition, many diseases also have a genetic component, meaning that genetics plays a role in the development of the condition, but it is a risk factor, and not the primary cause. That is, you can inherit a tendency to develop a certain disease.

- Infections: Diseases clearly caused by an infectious organism, which include viruses, bacteria, fungi, and protozoa. Some examples include pneumonia, meningitis, colds/flu, urinary tract infections, bone infections, tuberculosis, and HIV/AIDS.

- Trauma: A fall, automobile accident, or other physical trauma can cause brain hemorrhage, post-traumatic epilepsy, and brain injuries.

- Acquired physiologic errors: The majority of people who have disease have one or more that has been caused by acquired physiologic errors, or imbalances. Conditions such as heart disease, cancer, depression, arthritis, fibromyalgia, migraine, fatigue, ulcerative colitis, atherosclerosis, and many others fall into this category. This is the category of disease addressed by the Restorative Medicine approach.

Restorative Medicine treats the errors of physiology by restoring the body's hormones and nutrients to optimal levels. Normally, the body strives to keep a healthy ratio between different hormones. For example, some of the hormones that work together and for which we have identified an optimal ratio are DHEA and cortisol, and estrogen and progesterone. When hormone levels and ratios are not balanced, there is a breakdown in bodily functions.

Although we talk about hormones in much detail in Chapter 3, here we just want to say that critical hormones such as DHEA, pregnenolone, testosterone, and others begin to decline around age 35. Perhaps the most important thing that happens when hormone levels begin to decline is that the body tries to correct the problem by increasing production of cholesterol. To help prevent or correct this response and others launched by the body when hormone levels fall, the main goal of our Restorative Medicine Program is to bring a person's hormone levels back to what is optimal for each individual at age 25 to 30.

One Disease, One Treatment Approach

This Restorative Medicine approach is effective for the diseases and conditions caused by physiologic errors **because they are all basically the same disease.** This is a concept that shakes up many people because conventional medicine draws very clear distinctions between diseases. So how can heart disease be the same as migraine or arthritis or depression? **We propose that they are all fundamentally the same because they are caused by the same problem: an imbalance of our body's physiology, more specifically hormones and important vitamins and minerals.**

The concept is simple: all of nature wants to be in harmony. When it is not, it struggles to regain or restore equilibrium. In the human body, that struggle causes symptoms and laboratory abnormalities, which ultimately lead to a breakdown in bodily functions and natural defenses, and so manifests as disease. Many times these imbalances are silent, only showing themselves later on as a cancer or heart attack. Our Restorative Medicine Program is designed to correct that imbalance and stop the process in its tracks.

Howard's Story

Howard is a fifty-two-year-old management consultant who was seeing his primary care physician for high cholesterol and depression. He was also suffering with erectile dysfunction, which he had not discussed with his doctor. Howard was also experiencing problems with sleep, fatigue, and concentration.

Howard's doctor prescribed a statin for the high cholesterol, a selective serotonin reuptake inhibitor (SSRI) for the depressive mood, and a sleeping pill for the insomnia. After nearly six months of treatment, Howard's cholesterol had declined by only a few points (from 245 mg/dL to 240 mg/dL), he still felt depressed and tired most of the time, and his sleep had not improved much at all. The fact that he was still experiencing erectile dysfunction added to his down mood.

The problem with Howard's treatment program, as he learned when he came to see us, was that his doctor was treating symptoms, and treating them as if they were separate issues. His doctor didn't understand what we understand: that Howard essentially had one condition, and not five or six. Once we established Howard's hormone and lipid levels and developed a hormone restoration and nutrient supplement program for him, he leapt at the chance to change his life. Within a month his depression was gone, he was sleeping much better, and his sexual problem was "much improved." He also stopped taking the antidepressant and the sleeping pill. After three months of treatment, Howard's cholesterol was down to 210 mg/dL, and he decided to stop the statin as well.

Why did we succeed when Howard's doctor had not? Because we recognized and addressed Howard's one disease and treated it with the one approach that has worked time and time again.

Feeling "Old" versus Feeling Hormonal Decline

At sixty-two, Rebecca said she was "feeling her age." Her main complaints when she visited her doctor were fatigue, depression, lack of concentration, wrinkled skin, and problems with sleeping. She had passed through menopause by age fifty-five, and she said she felt like she had "never recovered" from the symptoms she had experienced. She was still working as a claims supervisor for a large company and for financial reasons needed to continue working for several more years, but she was concerned about her diminishing energy level.

We believe people don't feel their age; they feel the result of the decline in their hormone levels. When the amount of hormones and nutrients in the body are restored to optimal levels, people experience dramatic improvements in overall health and well-being. Some say they feel as if they have reversed the aging process, and in a sense they have, because their physiology is set as close as possible to that of a 29-year-old. Of course, you can't go back in time and be 29 forever, but you can achieve optimal quality of life, prevent disease, and effectively manage disease processes that may be present.

Because we are restoring hormones and overall body chemistry to optimal levels—and a decline in hormones has a negative impact on the quality, elasticity, and overall health of the skin—restorative medicine also helps preserve a more "youthful" look. Thus rather than "antiaging medicine," which is a popular term for this approach, we prefer to call it by its more accurate name of (Physiologic) Restorative Medicine. By restoring physiology we are in a sense restoring a more youthful state. The term "antiaging" implies that we are keeping you from getting older. Restorative Medicine is about making your body chemistry or physiology youthful. It's better than "antiaging."

As for Rebecca, she decided to try the Restorative Program, and within a few weeks she was feeling better. After several months, she said she now felt 'twenty years younger," her skin has improved, and she is looking forward to some vacations she previously had thought she would be too tired to enjoy.

What is our Restorative Medicine Program?

Our Restorative Medicine Program has a fundamental action plan designed to allow it to be highly individualized. It is clearly **not** a one-size-fits-all approach. The basic plan is this:

- A detailed history is gathered from patients and reviewed by the program's licensed medical physicians.

- Laboratory test data are collected and analyzed. The tests performed include: Lipid profile, complete blood count, chemistry panel, homocysteine levels, C-reactive protein, and levels of the following hormones: pregnenolone, DHEA sulfate, total testosterone, total estrogen (women), estradiol/total estrogen (men), progesterone, cortisol, TSH, T3, T4, prolactin, serotonin, melatonin, and Vitamin D, 25-Hydroxy. If needed, one or more of the following levels will also be taken (all described below): free testosterone, DHT, SHBG, PSA (men), and IGF-1. Again, one of the program's licensed medical physicians reviews the results. Each of the agents measured in these tests is explained below.

- Patients and physicians work together to devise a program of treatment that includes bioidentical hormones and natural vitamins and other supplements as indicated by the patient's test results, complaints, and history.

- At some point, patients are often asked to discontinue the medications they were taking when they entered the program. This is done in a coordinated manner between patients and their physicians. In many cases, patients are ready to stop taking their drugs within days of starting our Restorative Medicine Program.

- As patients embark on their Program, they can login on the Internet to learn about their program and to communicate with their program physician. This gives patients constant access to their program, laboratory results, advice, and progress. Communication regarding any problems, questions, or comments can be made immediately using this cyber approach.

What the Tests Mean

Before physicians can design an effective treatment plan for each patient, the results of the above-named tests need to be identified. Here is what each of the tests measures and what it means

- **Lipid profile:** A group of tests typically ordered together to determine a person's risk of coronary heart disease. The profile includes total cholesterol, high-density lipoprotein (HDL) cholesterol, low-density lipoprotein (LDL) cholesterol, and triglycerides.

- **Complete blood count (CBC):** A broad screening test that can check for anemia, infections, and many other diseases. The CBC examines different parts of the blood (e.g., white blood cells, red blood cells, hemoglobin, platelets), each of which has its own functions. Physicians order a CBC to establish a baseline for the various blood elements, to help diagnose symptoms, and to monitor disease and treatment. Significant elevations in white blood counts, for example, may confirm the presence of an infection and indicate that further testing is required to identify the cause. A platelet count that is very high or very low may confirm clotting or bleeding disorders.

- **Chemistry panel:** A group of tests that are routinely ordered to identify a person's general state of health, including electrolyte balance and/or the status of several major body organs. The tests are performed on a blood sample. There are two main panels: the Comprehensive Metabolic Panel, which contains 14 tests; and the Basic Metabolic Panel, which contains eight. We use the comprehensive panel.

- **Homocysteine level:** Homocysteine is an amino acid in the blood. Elevated levels are associated with an increased risk of stroke, atherosclerosis, heart disease, eye diseases, Alzheimer's disease and dementia, kidney disease, and erectile dysfunction. Dietary measures, especially certain B vitamins, have been shown to be effective in reducing homocysteine levels.

- **Pregnenolone:** A naturally occurring hormone that is the precursor for estrogens, progesterone, DHEA, cortisol, and testosterone. Optimal serum pregnenolone levels are 200 ng/dL for women and 180 ng/dL for men.

- **DHEA sulfate:** This test is done to evaluate the function of the adrenal glands. DHEA-sulfate (DHEA-S) is a hormone that is produced by the adrenal glands in both men and women. Elevated levels may indicate adrenal cancer, polycystic ovary syndrome, a tumor of the adrenal gland, or congenital adrenal hyperplasia.

The level of DHEA-S is also critical because it must be in balance with cortisol.

- **Total testosterone:** Testosterone is a steroid hormone produced by the testes in males and by the adrenal glands in both males and females and, in small amounts by the ovaries in females. The production of testosterone is stimulated and controlled by luteinizing hormone, which is made in the pituitary gland. A total testosterone value is taken to help explain erectile dysfunction, infertility, or premature or delayed puberty in males. High levels in men may indicate cancer of the adrenal glands or testicles. In women, abnormal levels may explain polycystic ovary syndrome, ovarian cancer, or an underactive pituitary gland.

- **Total estrogen:** Although there are more than 30 types of estrogen, this test measures the three mains ones: estrone (E1), 17beta-estradiol (E2), and estriol (E3). Estrone is the major estrogen after menopause. Estradiol is produced in women mainly in the ovaries and in the testes and adrenal glands in men. Estriol is the major estrogen whose level rises significantly during pregnancy.

- **Estradiol/total estrogen:** This test is taken to determine estrogen levels in men. Testosterone is converted into estrogen (estradiol) in men, so estrogen levels are important to determine.

- **Progesterone:** Levels of this hormone are used to help recognize and manage infertility, to determine or monitor ovulation, to diagnose an ectopic or failing pregnancy, and to determine the cause of abnormal uterine bleeding.

- **Cortisol:** This hormone is often called the stress hormone because blood levels rise when the body is exposed to physical or mental stress, vigorous activity, infection, or injury. Elevated levels may indicate problems with the adrenal or pituitary glands. It has a close relationship with DHEA-S.

- **TSH:** The thyroid stimulating hormone test is used to evaluate thyroid function and/or symptoms of hypothyroidism or hyperthyroidism; to diagnose and monitor female infertility; and evaluate pituitary gland function.

- **T3:** Triiodothyronine levels are checked for presence of overactive thyroid (hyperthyroidism) or low thyroid function (hypothyroidism) using a blood test.

- **T4:** Thyroxine levels are checked for presence of hyperthyroidism, hypothyroidism, and thyroid function in general.

- **C-reactive protein:** Normally there is no C-reactive protein in blood serum, and the presence of this protein is a sign that there is inflammation and/or an infection somewhere in the body. It can indicate rheumatoid arthritis, cancer, lupus, pneumonia, and other conditions.

- **Prolactin:** Levels of prolactin, a hormone produced by the pituitary gland, are measured when looking for pituitary tumors and for the cause of infertility, irregular periods, impotence, and milk production not related to breastfeeding (galactorrhea).

- **Serotonin:** This chemical is produced by nerve cells from foods that contain amino acids. Serotonin is found in the brain as well as in the blood and the digestive system. It regulates emotion and plays a major role in depression, anxiety, migraine, sexuality, and appetite.

- **Melatonin:** This hormone is produced by the pineal gland by converting tryptophan into serotonin. Melatonin is key in maintaining the sleep/wake cycle. Low levels can cause cortisol secretion to get out of balance.

- **Vitamin D, 25-Hydroxy:** Low levels of this hormone/vitamin are associated with bone loss, depression, fatigue, heart disease, and diabetes, among other conditions.

- **Free testosterone:** Testosterone is present in the blood as bound testosterone (about 97%) or as "free" testosterone (2-3%). Free testosterone is difficult to measure accurately and is often tested using the direct, radioimmunoassay method. High levels of free testosterone have been associated with better cognitive functioning.

- **DHT (dihydrotestosterone):** The active metabolite of testosterone, and three times more potent than testosterone.

- **SHBG (sex hormone binding globulin):** This test is used to evaluate the status of testosterone and estradiol. In men, a low testosterone level can cause infertility, erectile dysfunction, and reduced sex drive. In women, slightly elevated testosterone can cause infertility, acne, amenorrhea, and abnormal hair growth on the face (hirsutism). This test is usually ordered when total testosterone test results are not consistent with clinical signs, such as decreased sex drive in men or hirsutism in women.

- **PSA (prostate specific antigen):** Levels of this antigen are measured to identify possible prostate cancer. Normal value for total PSA is less than 4.0 ng/mL (nanograms per milliliter of blood). Men with a total PSA of 4.0 to 10.0 ng/mL are at increased risk (25% chance) of developing prostate cancer, benign prostate hypertrophy, or prostatitis. Those with a total PSA greater than 10.0 ng/mL have a 67 percent increased risk of developing prostate cancer.

- **IGF-1 (insulin-like growth factor):** Measured to determine pituitary function and the cause of any growth abnormalities.

Basic Restorative Medicine Approach

Physicians who provide our Restorative Medicine Program prescribe multiple bioidentical hormones in a customized manner, to simulate the optimal, natural human hormone production cycle upon which all organ systems such as the brain, skin, heart, immune system, bones and joints depend! Let's break this definition down into its parts.

Why are multiple hormones necessary? Because many hormones work together, and when you change the level of one you impact others. The goal is to achieve a balance of hormones, and this requires that you look at all the levels and make adjustments as needed.

Bioidentical vs Synthetic Hormones

Our Restorative Medicine Program is a **natural approach**, which means it uses hormones that are biochemically identical to those produced by the human body. Much controversy has revolved around the use of synthetic hormones, such as those derived from horse urine, for example (Premarin). Unfortunately many women still take this prescribed hormone therapy. (We discuss the problems with conventional hormone replacement therapy in Chapter 2.) The vitamins and other nutritional supplements that are part of our Restorative Medicine Program are also natural.

More than 10 years ago we employed the term hormonorestorative therapy into our practice for the regimen that was used for our patients. Hormonorestorative therapy was defined as multi-hormonal therapy with the use of a chemically identical formula to human hormones (so-called anthropo-identical) and is administered in physiologic ratios with dose schedules intended to simulate the natural human production cycle and allows for the restoration of an optimal level of hormones. The "optimal" was defined as a level of hormones in one third of the highest normal range from the testing laboratory for healthy 20-30 year old individuals for all steroid hormones (except estradiol/total estrogen for men). This level will result in youthful physiologic (not just "normal") levels and a patient without symptoms.

All of the hormones and nutritional supplements are prescribed to match the body's natural manufacturing and secretion cycles. Typically this means patients take a larger dose in the morning of their recommended therapy, and physicians recommend modifications according to a patient's needs and progress.

What does our Restorative Medicine Program Include?

Our Restorative Medicine Program typically involves taking basic hormones: pregnenolone, DHEA, triestrogen (women), progesterone, testosterone, hydrocortisone, Armour thyroid (a natural preparation containing T3 and T4 in the proper ratio), and melatonin. (Hormones are discussed in detail in Chapter 3.) This is just a general starting point: one of the beauties of our approach is that we customize a treatment plan for each individual based on his or her medical condition, test results, and needs.

In addition to the basic hormones, our Restorative Medicine Program may also include various nutritional and/or herbal supplements that help to restore important nutrients to optimal levels, to enhance the performance and efficiency of the hormones, and to resolve signs and symptoms the individual is experiencing. These also are explored in Chapter 3.

In some cases, we recommend that individuals make adjustments to their diet and/or add exercise to their lifestyle, but only after they have been on their programs for several months and hormonal balance has been restored. For many patients, losing weight is a goal, but the fact that they have been feeling depressed or unwell for so long has prevented them from effectively losing pounds through exercise and a healthful eating plan.

Now that you have a general idea of what our Restorative Medicine Program is about, we will turn to look at conventional medicine, and why it does not effectively treat or manage many of the most common medical conditions that affect humans.

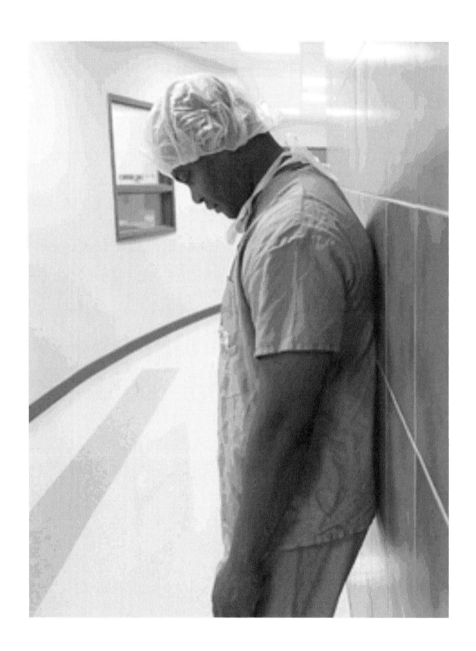

Chapter 2

WHY THE CURRENT MEDICINE MODEL DOESN'T WORK

Over a two-year period, Bernice had consulted with four doctors about her fatigue, insomnia, and migraines, but all they did was prescribe drugs for her head pain and sleeping pills for her insomnia. The only testing ordered by the doctors were a complete blood count and glucose testing, both of which did not show any significant values out of range. Yet none of the doctors ever checked her hormone levels or asked about her diet. After a year of experiencing two to three migraines per month and increasing insomnia and fatigue, this forty-four-year-old elementary school teacher could no longer keep up with the stress of her work. Bernice had to take a leave of absence and she became depressed. With a medicine cabinet full of prescriptions that were not offering her any lasting relief, Bernice felt at the end of her rope. When a friend told her about hormone restoration, Bernice contacted us almost immediately began treatment that included a balance of estrogens, progesterone, pregnenolone, melatonin, DHEA, and several nutrients. Within one month her fatigue and insomnia had decreased dramatically, and after three months her monthly migraines had disappeared, she was no longer depressed, and she was able to return to the classroom.

We can answer the implied question that is the title of this chapter in one succinct statement:

The current medicine model is flawed because it does not address the root causes of many diseases and health conditions.

The conventional medicine approach has several flaws. One is that it is largely drug-based. A major difference between a drug-driven system and bioidentical hormone restoration is that drugs—including synthetic hormones--are foreign invaders. Once these intruders are in the body, they set up new reactions that declare war on everything they touch; hormone restoration supplements that are bioidentical to the hormones produced naturally by the body are peace keepers that are sent in to restore normal, balanced physiological functions and systems.

In short, the current medical model applies temporary fixes to major, persistent health problems, and this approach ultimately does not serve the public. We believe there are also several other components of the conventional approach to medicine that are flawed and thus they contribute to the failure of mainstream medicine to allow the body to achieve a balanced, stable state of health and well-being.

The truth is, in recent years, an increasing number of people have been turning to nonpharmaceutical therapies because of their dissatisfaction with mainstream medicine, the lack of positive response to medications, the high costs of same, and the often overwhelming side effects associated with use of these medications. One of the main strengths of the Restorative Medicine Program is that it is effective without the use of drugs and their side effects.

With these thoughts in mind, in this chapter we look at the flaws inherent in the current system of medical care in contrast with our Restorative Medicine Program. We believe that having a better understanding of how mainstream medicine works and does not work can help individuals realize the limitations of the system and how to take better control of their health using alternative approaches that support balance and well-being.

Treat Symptoms, Not People

Although most people refer to the medical system in the United States as "health care," a more accurate phrase would be "putting out fires." Most of the effort put forth by members of the mainstream medical community is channeled into managing and treating disease, rather than preventing it. In 2008, $2.1 trillion was spent in the United States on medical care, and 95 percent of that money was spent to treat diseases that had already developed. Of that money, 75 percent or more was spent on treating diseases that are preventable or reversible, including heart disease, diabetes, obesity, and stroke.

The Power of Prevention

Perhaps the most impressive study about the power of prevention is the INTERHEART study. This Canadian-led global study involved following approximately 30,000 adults on six continents to identify risk factors for acute myocardial infarction (heart attack). The results of the study were published in September 2004 in *The Lancet,* and in essence the investigators found that the risk factors were the same in nearly every geographic region and every racial/ethnic group around the world. They named nine easily measured and modifiable risk factors (smoking, lipids [cholesterol, triglycerides], hypertension, diabetes, abdominal obesity, diet, physical activity, alcohol use, and psychosocial factors) that account for more than 90 percent of the risk of heart attack.

The point here is that all of these risk factors are **modifiable,** which means people have the power to significantly reduce their risk of heart attack if they heed these risk factors. Yet the reality is that obesity and diabetes are epidemics in the United States. The majority of people do not eat a healthful diet nor get enough physical exercise. According to the National Center for Health Statistics, less than one-third (31%) of adults in the United States participate in regular leisure physical activity, and 39.5 percent do not engage in such physical activity at all. Despite all the scientific evidence about the deadly nature of smoking, about 19 percent of Americans still light up, according to the Centers for Disease Control and Prevention. The American Heart Association reports that about 73.6 million Americans age 20 and older have high blood pressure: that's one-third of adults in the United States. High cholesterol affects 42 million Americans, and an additional 63 million have borderline high cholesterol levels.

Let's look at heart disease as an example of how mainstream medicine treats symptoms rather than people, and how a strong emphasis on prevention could prevent millions of invasive procedures and deaths. In 2006, surgeons performed 1.3 million coronary angioplasties and 448,000 coronary bypass surgeries, for a total cost of more than $100 billion. Yet these procedures are not even helpful in most cases. According to a study published in April 2007 in the *New England Journal of Medicine,* coronary bypass surgery extends the life of less than 3 percent of patients who undergo the procedure, and angioplasties are not effective in preventing heart attack in stable patients, who make up 95 percent of those who have the operation.

Medicare and insurance companies continue to spend billions of dollars to put out fires, yet they allocate little or no money for prevention or integrative medicine, or for successful restorative hormone therapy. We hope that this injustice will change some day soon, as do the millions of people who seek integrative and preventive care.

Fighting Injustice

This brings to mind the fight being fought by one of our clients, Arlene, of Missouri, who is challenging this injustice with her insurance company. Arlene is a forty-five-year-old woman who came to see us after suffering from migraines for 20 years, depression for 17 years, and constipation for 15 years. She experienced her first migraine after the birth of her first child at age 24, and thereafter she usually had two migraines each month: one at ovulation and the other when her period started, although others would occur frequently as well. She also suffered with occasional sinus headaches. For two decades she used various medications, but none of them provided any significant relief. She laments the "many days, weeks, months...lost due to those awful attacks."

Arlene started her Program on July 26, 2007, and five months later, she had had only three migraines, and each of them was only 25 percent as painful as they once had been. She also no longer needed the daily antidepressants she had been prescribed over the past 17 years. Because of chronic constipation, Arlene had a rectal prolapse in 2005 and had 18 inches of her intestinal tract removed. Subsequent problems with her small intestine and postsurgical complications required three more surgeries, all in 2005. Since starting her Program, her chronic constipation has disappeared as well.

Over the years, Arlene had always felt that her migraines, constipation, depression, and sinus headaches were all related, but that possibility had never been validated by any physician until she discovered us. Arlene's "beef" with her insurance company revolves around the fact that while her insurance carrier was willing enough to pay for years and years of prescription drugs, hospitalizations, surgeries, and doctor visits, all of which treated symptoms but never provided her with any meaningful relief, the insurance company had refused to pay for the three-month program—the treatment that was successful for her. She notes that her Program "has helped me get my health back....This is the only treatment that has actually attacked the cause of the migraines and given me such relief!"

Lack of Nutritional Support

Doesn't it seem curious that the women and men who study to become physicians are provided very little training in food and nutrition, yet the public expects them to provide sage advice about the very fuel that makes—or breaks—the body? Research shows that medical students say they are inadequately trained in nutrition during medical school, and once they get into practice, they don't have much confidence if they need to discuss nutritional issues with their patients. Thus nutritional training needs to be an integral part of the education in medical schools and residency programs, and in some schools this is happening.

However, in the meantime, we have several generations of practicing physicians who are not well-versed in nutrition. At the same time, the number of people who have chronic diseases in which diet plays a key role continues to rise. Obesity, type 2 diabetes, cardiovascular disease, hypertension, and high cholesterol, among others, affect a staggering number of adults and an increasing number of children, who will carry these medical legacies with them into adulthood.

Although there is much evidence that diet and lifestyle modifications can prevent these diseases and in some cases reverse them, the current medicine model is to prescribe medications when patients have a complaint: pills to help you lose weight, to lower cholesterol, to reduce blood pressure, to sleep, to wake up, to feel less blue, to improve sex drive. Naturally, prescription drugs and weight-loss products are billion-dollar industries, so there is a financial incentive to keep demand for them strong.

Our Restorative Medicine Program acknowledges the importance of nutritional balance in overall health. While hormone restoration is the hallmark of our Program, nutritional balance is also key and is selectively built into each person's treatment plan. One of the truly rewarding aspects of our work is that, along with the relief people get once they follow their Program that is developed for them, many of them also suddenly want to take better care of their health: they improve their diet, adopt an exercise program, lose weight, improve their strength, and enhance their health overall. As some of our patients have told us, once they are in balance internally, they want to extend that balance to encompass all of their being, and so they eat better and become more physically active.

A Drug-Based Approach

We are a drug-loving society. We turn to prescription and over-the-counter pills and other forms of medication to help us lose weight, treat the sniffles, relieve the blues, fight pain, reduce triglycerides, and raise "good" cholesterol. We take pills to help prevent the heartburn that comes after eating a large bowl of extra hot chili and then another pill to ease the indigestion. We take pills to lift us up, others to let us down.

The problem is, prescription and over-the-counter drugs don't treat disease, they just put a bandage or salve on the symptoms. Most physicians care for disease, not health. Thus the use of pharmaceuticals is the hallmark of mainstream medicine, and doctors dispense 4 billion prescriptions per year in the United States. Like all things in life, there is a time and place for everything. When it comes to medications, there is judicious use and nonjudicious use. Our experience has been that, when treating a great number of the most common medical conditions like those covered in this book, pharmaceuticals may not be the safe or effective path to take.

Why Drugs Fail: An Example

A good example of the failure of drugs to effectively and safely treat a serious medical condition is statins. Statins are a class of drugs used to treat hypercholesterolemia—high cholesterol. As of 2008, statins were the best-selling prescription drugs in the world, with $20 billion sold per year in the United States alone. Although many studies show that statins provide primary prevention, the long-term tolerability of these drugs is highly questionable. Statins can reduce total cholesterol in the blood and thus help decrease the incidence of coronary heart disease, but the use of statins is also associated with muscle pain and weakness, dizziness, cognitive impairment, peripheral neuropathy, and an increased risk of noncardiovascular death.

For example, when we review the results of major primary prevention trials, we find that the 15 percent decrease in deaths from heart disease in patients who were using cholesterol-lowering drugs (CLD) is offset by increases in deaths from other conditions. One area of concern is cancer: Two popular classes of CLDs—fibrates and statins—cause cancer and liver damage in rodents. A significant increase in cancer incidence, especially gastrointestinal cancer, has been seen in people who take CLDs. Use of CLDs also increases cancer at the expense of decreasing deaths from cardiovascular conditions, especially among the elderly and people who are being treated with immunotherapy for cancer. There is also evidence of a relationship between cancer and statin dosing. Yet another area of concern is stroke. Low or reduced levels of serum cholesterol have been shown to increase the risk of death from hemorrhagic stroke.

Impact of Drugs on Hormones

Although we have not yet fully explained the major role hormones play in restorative medicine, here we want to point out the potentially devastating impact the use of drugs can have on hormone levels and balance in the human body. Studies show that cholesterol-lowering drugs, for example, can cause hormone level abnormalities. Some research indicates that statin use disturbs testosterone levels, while specific drugs seem to target certain hormones. The statin mevastatin, for example, can significantly decrease production of progesterone and testosterone, while clofibrate has a similar effect on testosterone and cortisol.

At an even more basic level, the use of synthetic hormones, rather than bioidentical hormones, can disrupt the body's natural hormone balance. The human body contains all the elements it needs to process natural hormones when they occur in their natural proportions. When we introduce synthetic hormones, the human body does not metabolize them in the same way it does bioidentical hormones. That's because synthetic hormones are not hormones; like drugs, they are foreign substances.

The Trouble with Cholesterol-Lowering Drugs

- The range of side effects caused by CLDs ranges from 4 to 38 percent in many studies, but has been seen to rise as high as nearly 75 percent in some trials (especially for cerivastatin and pravastatin).

- Most patients who begin cholesterol-lowering therapy stop it within one year: studies show 60 percent of patients discontinued their medication over 12 months, and only about 33 percent of patients ever reach their treatment goals.

- The most common side effects of CLDs are abdominal pain, chest pain, dizziness, asthenia/fatigue, fibromyalgia, headache, insomnia, elevated transaminase levels in the liver, upper respiratory tract infection; also eczema, rashes, cramps, exercise intolerance, severe rhabdomyolysis, renal failure, and poor quality of life.

- Statins deplete coenzyme Q10, a substance that is important for heart health. Supplementation with CoQ10 should be pursued to offset the dangers of statin drugs to the heart.

- Statins may impair heart pumping function due to their myopathic effects.

- Other conditions that may occur as a result of taking statins include erectile dysfunction, dementia, memory loss, severe irritability, peripheral neuropathy, restlessness, lupus-like syndrome, pleurisy, arthralgia, tachyphylaxis, and mental confusion.

Conventional Hormone Replacement Therapy

The main problem with conventional hormone replacement therapy is that it uses drugs, not hormones, even though the pharmaceutical companies call them hormones. Consider Premarin, which is conjugated equine (horse) estrogens derived from the urine of pregnant horses. It is composed of at least ten different estrogens, along with some androgens and progestins. This product is not bioidentical to the hormones found in the human body.

Interestingly, sales of Premarin fell dramatically after the Women's Health Initiative found that hormone replacement therapy was associated with an increased risk of breast cancer, heart disease, deep vein thrombosis, and stroke. Yet after several years of trepidation by women and physicians, sales began to rise again, and in 2008 they increased 15 percent over the previous year to a total of $276 million.

Other problems associated with conventional hormone replacement therapy are covered in Chapter 3, where we discuss the individual hormones.

Lack of Knowledge about Bioidentical Hormones

Many physicians and other health care practitioners believe that hormones may cause clotting disturbances as well as breast cancer, prostate cancer, or other cancers that have a hormone component. Yet these fears are unfounded if the true definition of hormones is applied: substances that the body produces naturally to regulate itself. When this definition is used, we find that no studies have shown that hormones cause any of these health issues.

The problem is that pharmaceutical companies produced drugs—and yet they call them hormones--to replace naturally produced hormones. These are the same hormones/drugs that are used in the majority of scientific studies and the ones that have been implicated in the development of cancers and clotting disturbances. However, again, these are drugs, not hormones. Natural bioidentical hormones have not been shown to cause cancer.

For example, conventional doctors have long held that testosterone therapy leads to an increased risk of prostate cancer, and so they are hesitant about prescribing testosterone to men. Yet an increasing amount of research, especially from Harvard-based Abraham Morgentaler, MD, FACS, shows some very important results:

- High blood levels of testosterone do not increase the risk of prostate cancer, they decrease the risk of prostate cancer

- Low blood levels of testosterone do not protect against prostate cancer, they actually increase the risk.

- Testosterone therapy does not increase the risk of prostate cancer, even among men who are at high risk for the disease.

Another example comes from the use of progesterone, a wonderful hormone necessary in both males and females. Studies indicate that the synthetic replacement drug progestin increases the risk of breast cancer and blood clots.

As you may have guessed, natural progesterone causes blood to flow more freely and does not increase the risk of breast cancer.

What Happened To "Do No Harm"?

According to HealthGrades' fifth annual Patient Safety in American Hospitals Study, medical errors cost Medicare $8.8

billion and resulted in 238,337 potentially preventable deaths during 2004 through 2006. Note that these are just **Medicare** figures. An Institute of Medicine report in April 2006 stated that each year about 1.5 million Americans are harmed by medication mistakes made in US hospitals, and 7,000 of these Americans die due to the error. Overall, about 106,000 people die per year due to negative effects of drugs, 80,000 die due to infections acquired while in the hospital, and 12,000 die due to unnecessary surgery.

Although these figures are discouraging, many health care professionals believe they are underestimated. These figures—and indeed many available research studies—do not reflect the estimated hundreds of thousands of people who have stopped seeking medical treatment because it has failed them. Nor does it include people who have been misdiagnosed or never diagnosed. The figures also do not tell the stories of people who are ill or who die because they never received proper information and instruction on preventive measures, including health screenings and nutritional support.

And there's more. According to a 2008 study by New York's The Commonwealth Fund, US patients experienced the highest medical errors, coordination problems, and out-of-pocket expenses than seven other countries (Australia, Britain, Canada, France, Germany, the Netherlands, and New Zealand). Fifty-four percent of chronically ill patients in the United States did not get recommended care, see a doctor, or fill prescriptions because of costs, compared with 7 to 36 percent in other countries.

Isn't it clear that there must be a better way?

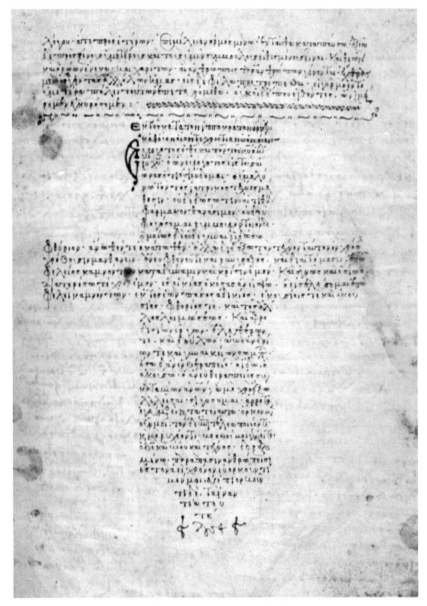

12th Century Hippocratic Oath

Chapter
3

THE RESTORATIVE PLAYERS:
HORMONES AND NUTRIENTS

The best thing about my Restorative Medicine Program—besides the fact that it works—is that everything I take is natural. I stopped taking the drugs I had been prescribed, and now I just take a few natural hormones and several nutrients, and I'm good to go. Gone are the fatigue, depression, menopausal symptoms, and muscle pain that plagued me for more than a decade. I'm like a new woman!"

Pamela, forty-four-year-old banker

In this chapter, we introduce you to the hormones and nutrients that are part of our Restorative Medicine Program. We discuss what each element is, its function, and how the various hormones and nutrients work independently and together in balance for health and well-being.

What are Hormones?

Hormones are chemical substances that are manufactured by specialized glands or tissues which produce and secrete them on demand. It's been said that hormones are the ultimate messengers: these complex chemicals transport information from the brain to the glands, from the glands to the cells, and from the cells to the brain, so they truly have access to every part of the body.

The word "hormone" is derived from the Greek word *hormo*, which means "to set in motion." That's exactly what hormones do: they regulate, stimulate, and control an endless list of critical tasks and functions, depending on their origin. Most of the body's hormones are produced by the glands of the endocrine system, which includes hypothalamus, pituitary gland, pineal gland, the thyroid, adrenal glands, ovaries, and testes. These hormones are sent directly to the bloodstream. Other hormones are produced by the mucous membranes of the small intestine and the placenta. The hormones that are the focus of our Restorative Medicine Program include some of the ones manufactured by the endocrine glands, such as pregnenolone, estrogen, testosterone, progesterone, DHEA, cortisol, melatonin, and thyroid hormones and, to a lesser extent, insulin. We also pay a lot of attention to serotonin. Serotonin is a hormone manufactured by the body and found in the brain, pineal gland, bloodplatelets, and digestive tract. It plays a critical role in making blood vessels constrict and in supporting normal mood. Serotonin is also a neurotransmitter, which means it helps nerves communicate with each other.

Hormones are classified into two groups based on their chemical makeup: peptides, which are derivatives of amino acids; and steroids. Most hormones are peptides and are produced by the anterior pituitary, thyroid, parathyroid, placenta, and pancreas. Steroid hormones are synthesized from cholesterol and then modified through a series of chemical reactions to form hormones that are designed to perform a variety of functions. They are secreted by the adrenal glands, ovaries, and testes (see box, "Major Classes of Steroid Hormones").

If you look at the chart, you can see how a decline in the production of pregnenolone, which occurs with age, has a direct impact on the production and level of other hormones. All of the hormones in this chart are among the ones we are concerned with in our Restorative Medicine Program.

Steroid Hormone Production

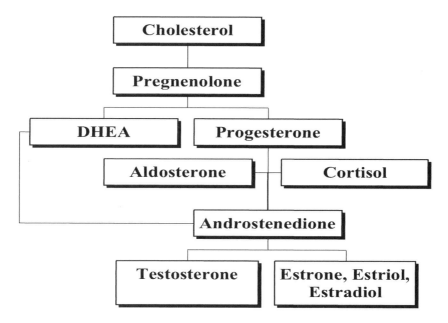

Major Classes of Steroid Hormones

- Progestagens: Progesterone is the main hormone in this class. Both men and women have this hormone, although males have much lower levels.

- Glucocorticoids: These are antistress hormones, which include cortisol and cortisone.

- Mineralocorticoids: Aldosterone is in this class, and it is responsible for regulating potassium and sodium levels.

- Androgens: These are the male sex hormones, of which testosterone is the main hormone. Females also have this hormone, but typically at low levels.

- Estrogen: This is one of the primary female sex hormones, of which the three most important types are estradiol, estriol, and estrone. Males have low levels of estrogen, specifically estradiol.

The Decline in Hormone Levels

Experts have known for many years that hormone levels decline as people age, but it has also become increasingly evident that as hormone levels decrease, people age. So which comes first, the chicken or the egg? Do people age because their hormone levels fall, or do levels decline because people age?

Hormone levels are believed to be at their optimal and most potent levels when people are 25 to 30 years of age. After age 30, hormone levels begin to decline with each passing year as the glands that produce them gradually lose their ability to manufacture and secrete them. Yet the irony is, it is during these advancing years that people most need optimal levels of hormones, to enjoy and maintain health and well-being and to prevent disease. These are the years when people are typically building and advancing in their careers and starting and raising a family.

Our Restorative Medicine Program offers a safe, individually tailored program that restores hormones and nutrients to youthful levels, both to help prevent and/or treat disease, and to restore and maintain health and well-being.

Bioidentical vs Non-bioidentical Hormones

Supplemental hormones are available in two forms: bioidentical and non-bioidentical. As we noted in the beginning of this book, bioidentical hormones are biochemically the same as those that the body produces naturally. This means that the molecular shape, structure, and make-up are identical, and indeed they must be, so they can unlock the body's hormone receptor sites. Bioidentical or "natural" hormones are made in the laboratory in a process called synthesizing. Bioidentical hormones are the cornerstone of our Program.

Non-bioidentical hormones are the form typically used by conventional medical professionals. (Some people refer to this form of hormones as "synthetic," but because both bioidentical and non-bioidentical hormones are synthesized—made in the laboratory--we use the term *non-bioidentical* to avoid confusion*). One of the most well-known, non-bioidentical hormone products is Premarin (generic name, conjugated equine estrogen), which is made from pregnant mares' (horse) urine. The percentages of horse estrone and estradiol in Premarin are much greater than the amounts the body produces, and thus use of this drug can result in hormone imbalance. In addition, Premarin contains estrogen that is unique to horses—of course.

The 1995 Nurses' Health Study, which is one of the largest studies ever done, found that women who took non-bioidentical estrogen alone had a 36 percent increased risk of breast cancer. Women who took non-bioidentical estrogen plus progestin (which is also non-bioidentical) had a 50 percent increase risk, while those who took progestins alone had a 240 percent increase of breast cancer. **Bioidentical hormones do not involve such risks!**

The Neurohormonal System

Our introduction of hormones and our Restorative Medicine Program would not be complete without a discussion of the basis of the Program—the neurohormonal system. This network of hormones, hormone messengers, hormone receptors, and nerve pathways works in synch to maintain balance among the various organs and systems in the body. A key component of the neurohormonal system is the hypothalamic-pituitary-adrenal axis, or HPA axis, and its relationship with steroid hormones. A basic knowledge of the HPA axis can help you better understand how our Restorative

Medicine Program can work to improve your health and that of your loved ones. Let's look at each of the components of the HPA axis and how they interact.

HPA-Axis Diagram

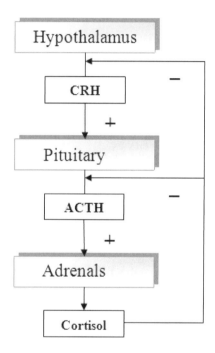

Hypothalamus

The hypothalamus is a tiny site deep in the brain that acts as the control center for most of the body's hormonal systems and the regulator of homeostasis, which is a stable state of equilibrium. For example, the hypothalamus determines how much cortisol the body needs when it is in a stressful situation. To meet that need, it produces corticotropin-releasing hormone (CRH), which travels to the pituitary gland, where it binds to specific receptors on cells in the gland. The gland then produces another hormone, adreno-corticotropic hormone (ACTH). The ACTH travels to the adrenal gland, where it stimulates the production of adrenal hormones. The adrenals increase their secretion of cortisol, which then initiates actions that will alleviate the harmful effects of stress through negative feedback to the hypothalamus and the pituitary, which decreases the concentration of ACTH and cortisol in the blood when the stress subsides. The pituitary also releases beta-endorphin, a morphine-like substance that reduces pain.

Pituitary Gland

This pea-sized gland is located at the base of the brain and is attached to the hypothalamus by nerve fibers. The pituitary gland is divided into two distinct lobes, and each one produces specific hormones when prompted by the hypothalamus. In addition to ACTH, the pituitary also secretes follicle-stimulating hormone (FSH), which travels to the ovaries and stimulates the development of follicles, tiny sacs that contain eggs. FSH also stimulates the secretion of estradiol and thus has an impact on the amount of estrogen that the body needs to balance against progesterone.

Luteinizing hormone (LH), another pituitary hormone, stimulates secretion of testosterone in the testes in males and in the ovaries in females, where the testosterone is then converted into estrogen. The pituitary also produces thyroid-stimulating hormone (TSH), which in turn stimulates the thyroid gland to secrete the hormones thyroxine (T4) and triiodothyronine (T3). Both of these hormones are involved in the optimal functioning of the thyroid gland.

Adrenal Glands

Now we move away from the brain to the top of the kidneys, where the adrenal glands are located. Each adrenal is composed of an inner part (medulla) and outer part (cortex), which itself consists of three zones. Each of the zones contains cholesterol and an enzyme called P450 scc (or 20,22-Desmolase), which converts the cholesterol into pregnenolone with the assistance of other enzymes. Here's a breakdown of each zone:

- Zona glomerulosa produces aldosterone, a mineralocorticoid that regulates the sodium:potassium ratio in the blood, which impacts blood volume and blood pressure

- Zona reticularis produces progesterone, DHEA, DHEA-S, and small amounts of testosterone and estrogens.

- Zona fasciculate produces cortisol, a stress hormone. Insufficient production of cortisol can cause headache, gastrointestinal problems, fatigue, dizziness, and low blood glucose (sugar), among other symptoms.

Because the adrenal glands play such a critical role in hormone production, it is essential that they function optimally. When they don't—and this is a common problem known as adrenal fatigue or adrenal insufficiency—people are susceptible to a long list of signs and symptoms. Adrenal insufficiency occurs when the adrenal glands are overworked or damaged, usually associated with chronic stress. Such stress can include having to work everyday at a job you dislike to having a chronic infection, lack of sleep, high intake of sugar or caffeine, financial worries, exposure to environmental toxins (e.g., second hand smoke, gas fumes), or feeling like you have to "do it all."

Adrenal insufficiency sneaks up on you. Over time, chronic stress causes the adrenals to produce large amounts of cortisol and adrenaline. Simultaneously, DHEA production declines. For a while, cortisol and adrenaline production remains high, then it returns to normal. To compensate for the reduced production of cortisol and adrenaline, the body reduces its production of pregnenolone, which in turn reduces the manufacture of DHEA, progesterone, estrogens, and testosterone in favor of cortisol. Eventually, however, the adrenals breakdown, cortisol and adrenaline levels are depleted, and severe hormonal imbalances among the steroid hormones occurs.

Indications that you may have adrenal insufficiency include insomnia, fatigue (especially in the morning and between 3 and 5 PM when cortisol levels fall), impaired memory and concentration, indigestion, anxiety, chronic pain, unexplained hair loss, poor blood sugar control, depression, reduced sex drive, and alternating diarrhea and constipation.

Adrenal insufficiency is often missed by conventional doctors, and one reason is that adrenal hormone levels in people who have this condition often are considered to be "normal," even though they can be about half of the optimum level. The misconception that such low levels are "normal" results in a missed diagnosis in many people, especially women.

Restoring Hormone Balance

We have talked a lot about optimal hormone levels, but the other equally important part of the hormone picture is balance. It is critical to achieve and maintain a balanced ratio between hormones that complement each other, such as progesterone and estrogen, and cortisol and DHEA, rather than restore individual hormones to optimal numbers. Only when all the selected hormones are restored to levels that achieve hormonal balance, and ratios that are specific to each individual's unique body chemistry, can we effectively treat that person's disease or medical condition and their whole being.

Sometimes patients ask if they can take just one or two hormones instead of the four or five that may be indicated by their test results. The answer is no: when we restore all the complementary hormones, we not only achieve balance, we also can use the lowest dosages of hormones and other supplements possible because we have better control over the entire restoration process. When we have control over the balancing act, patients can gain control of their health.

Reference vs Optimal Ranges of Hormones

Throughout this book you will see the terms "reference range" and "optimal range" when we talk about hormones, test results, and dosing. Reference range is a set of values that conventional medical professionals use to interpret test results. The range is usually based on values that represent 95 percent of the normal population. References ranges vary, because they depend on the age, sex, and race of the population, as well as the instruments that are used to test the levels. We believe reference ranges present several significant problems, including the fact that the "average" person in today's society is more likely to be malnourished, overstressed, and overweight, which does not provide a healthful baseline. Another problem is that the ranges are too broad to be useful in identifying health problems or recommending treatment for individual patients.

Yet another problem is that reference ranges are age specific. A sixty-year-old man, for example, who has erectile dysfunction, fatigue, and insomnia, may be told by his physician that his hormone levels are within reference or "normal" range, yet the levels that are optimal for his health are typically outside that range.

That's why we use optimal ranges of hormone levels for our Program. Optimal ranges are those seen in healthy twenty- to thirty-year-old men and women, and are the ones required to maintain good health. Since our Restorative Medicine Program is designed to restore each patient's hormone levels to his or her optimal range, we are always mindful that every individual functions best at levels that are unique to him or her. Therefore, reference ranges and optimal ranges are guidelines only, and not absolute levels to be achieved (see box).

Typically, however, we find that all basic hormones must be at or close to optimal levels to effectively treat or eliminate an individual's health challenges. Yet, as you can see in the table of "Reference and Optimal Ranges for Hormones," the low end of what conventional medicine considers to be within its reference or "normal" range is significantly lower than the lowest end of the optimal range. This shows clearly that a state of deficiency is deemed "normal" by mainstream medicine, which leads to a need for drugs.

Hormone	Reference Range	Optimal Range
Total Cholesterol	< 200 mg/dL	170-200 mg/dL
Total Estrogen (Females Only)	61-437 pg/mL	250-437 pg/mL
Estradiol (Males Only)	0-53 pg/mL	<25 pg/mL
Progesterone:		
Females:	0.2-28 ng/mL	6-28 ng/mL
Males:	0.3-1.2 ng/mL	1-1.2 ng/mL
Total Testosterone		
Females:	14-76 ng/dL	60-76 ng/dL
Males:	241-827 ng/dL	650-827 ng/dL
DHEA-Sulfate		
Females:	65-380 ug/dL	250-380 ug/dL
Males:	280-640 ug/dL	500-640 ug/dL
Pregnenolone		
Females:	10-230 ng/dL	200-230 ng/dL
Males:	10-200 ng/dL	180-200 ng/dL
Cortisol (a.m.)	4.3-22.4 ug/dL	15-22.4 ug/dL

Pregnenolone

Pregnenolone may not be a hormone you are familiar with or have even heard of before, but it is critically important because it is the precursor to other naturally occurring hormones, including those that are at the heart of our Restorative Medicine Program. More and more physicians are recognizing the importance of restoring youthful levels of these hormones (i.e., estrogen, progesterone, testosterone, cortisol, DHEA), yet pregnenolone is nearly always ignored.

Benefits of Pregnenolone

In the body, pregnenolone is made directly from cholesterol (see figure p.39), while the bioidentical pregnenolone used in our Restorative Medicine Program is created from wild yams (*Dioscorea villosa*) and is bioidentical to the hormone produced by the human body. This hormone performs many critical functions in the body, including:

- Fights the effects of fatigue and stress. Studies conducted with students, pilots, and workers found that pregnenolone can enhance job performance, reduce the impact of stress, and improve feelings of well-being.

- Relieves arthritis pain. Several studies show pregnenolone helps improve joint pain and joint mobility.

- Protects against coronary artery disease and improves heart health. Restoring pregnenolone to youthful levels can reduce cholesterol levels.

- Boosts the immune system and increases energy level.

- Enhances mood and relieves depressive symptoms. Daily doses of pregnenolone have improved mood in some individuals.

- Promotes healthy brain function and protects against dementia, including Alzheimer's disease. Animal studies suggest pregnenolone could prevent age-related cognitive disturbances and also help regulate function of the nervous system. Pregnenolone increases the release of acetylcholine, a neurotransmitter that plays a major role in memory, cognition, and sleep.

Taking Pregnenolone

The optimal serum levels of pregnenolone are considered to be 180 nanograms per deciliter (ng/dL) for men and 200 ng/dL for women. Supplements of pregnenolone are available in capsule form and as a sublingual tablet. A typical dosage is 50 to 200 mg daily, taken in the morning on an empty stomach, although we determine doses individually to meet each person's needs.

Pregnenolone is considered to be safe even at high doses. However, because pregnenolone is converted into DHEA and progesterone, which are then converted into other hormones, we recommend periodic blood testing of hormones to monitor levels and ratios to ensure no imbalances are created.

DHEA

Dehydroepiandrosterone (DHEA) is produced and secreted mainly by the adrenal glands and is the most common steroid hormone in the body. It is metabolized from pregnenolone and acts as a precursor to other sex hormones, including estrogens and testosterone. It has a close relationship with cortisol (see "Cortisol").

DHEA levels begin to decline naturally in the body after age 30, but they can also be depleted if you take various drugs, including insulin, opiates, and corticosteroids. Women tend to have lower levels of DHEA than men, and they also lose the hormone more quickly as they age. The body's production of DHEA is identified by measuring the amount of DHEA sulfate (DHEA-S) in a blood sample. As we noted in Chapter 1, DHEA-S is measured as part of a basic steroid hormone panel.

The body's natural production cycle of DHEA works like this: the adrenal glands produce the hormone early in the day, and then the liver converts it to DHEA-S. The DHEA-to-DHEA-S ratio typically reaches its optimal balance of 10 percent DHEA and 90 percent DHEA-S.

Benefits of DHEA

Maintaining a balanced level of DHEA in the body offers many benefits, including:

- Improves heart health and lowers blood cholesterol levels. Studies show a clear relationship between declining DHEA levels and cardiovascular disease in both men and women. DHEA also has been shown to protect against development of atherosclerosis and coronary artery disease.

- Delays onset or slows the progression of diabetes

- Improves arthritis symptoms

- Helps reverse declining mental acuity. People with Alzheimer's disease have elevated levels of cortisol and imbalanced cortisol/DHEA ratios. DHEA restoration may balance this ratio and protect mental capacities.

- Protects bone density

- Has some anti-cancer properties

Generally, low levels of DHEA are associated with heart disease, diabetes, inflammation, arthritis, lupus, Alzheimer's disease, and other diseases. More specifically, in menopausal women, a decline in DHEA levels has been associated with a decline in libido, strength, muscle mass, bone density, and energy.

Supplementation with DHEA can improve several aspects of the immune system, including reducing inflammation associated with arthritis, heart disease, and lupus. Studies show that among postmenopausal women, taking DHEA can improve mood, sexual desire and enjoyment, and increase bone mineral density. In men, DHEA restoration therapy complements testosterone therapy, and in fact helps raise the blood levels of free testosterone, which is the active form.

How Safe is DHEA?

Whenever we talk about DHEA, invariably someone will ask whether supplementing with this hormone increases the risk of getting cancer, specifically breast and prostate cancer, two cancers that may be hormone-driven. DHEA may be converted into estrogen, which is why women with breast cancer are often advised not to use DHEA, while men with prostate cancer or severe benign prostate disease are typically advised to avoid DHEA because it can be converted into testosterone.

Our research shows that DHEA actually protects against breast cancer, as well as cancer of the skin, colon, liver, and thyroid. Remember how we have emphasized the importance of restoring levels of all the hormones and not just one? DHEA is safe because we simultaneously restore the two basic female hormones—estrogen and progesterone—to optimal levels, and also block the conversion of testosterone to dihydrotestosterone (DHT), the biologically active metabolite of testosterone that is associated with prostate enlargement and hair loss.

We also recommend that patients take 7-keto DHEA, which is another metabolite of DHEA. A major difference between 7-keto DHEA and DHEA is that 7-keto does not convert to estrogen and testosterone. This means patients can take a lower dose of DHEA, which helps to balance estrogen and progesterone and to keep cortisol levels at optimal levels, and it also reduces or eliminates the risk of experiencing side effects.

DHEA Supplements

DHEA supplements are generally well tolerated and cause minimal side effects. The starting dose for most people is between 15 and 100 mg taken in one daily dose on an empty stomach, about 30 minutes before breakfast. DHEA is best taken early in the morning because this timing simulates the body's natural DHEA cycle. Sometimes an additional smaller afternoon dose of DHEA is required. Ideal serum reference ranges of DHEA-S are 500 to 640 ug/dL for men and 250 to 380 ug/dL for women. Because everyone reacts differently to DHEA supplementation, we recommend monitoring blood levels regularly to make sure the proper balance is achieved and maintained. Once the hormonal level of DHEA has been restored, it is necessary to continue taking the supplement to maintain an optimal blood level.

In women, doses of DHEA greater than 50 to 100 mg daily may cause "male" traits, including the development of facial hair, oily skin, or acne. These symptoms will disappear once the dose of DHEA is decreased.

Estrogen

The word "estrogen" is a general term for about 30 different types of the hormone, but we focus on the three most common—estradiol, estriol, and estrone. Estrogen is usually referred to as a female hormone because it plays such major roles in menstruation, pregnancy, breast development, and bone health, among other essential functions, but it is a critical hormone in men as well.

Estrogen in Women

The fact that women have more than three hundred different types of estrogen receptors throughout the body is proof that this hormone has a major impact on many different aspects of health. Keeping the three estrogens in proper balance with each other and with other steroid hormones—especially progesterone (see "Decline in Progesterone/Estrogen Dominance")--is essential for health and well-being. When estrogen levels decline, women typically experience hot flashes, irritability, vaginal dryness, sleep problems, poor memory, and night sweats. When estrogen levels are elevated or the estrogen/progesterone balance is unbalanced and estrogen is dominant (see "Decline in Progesterone/Estrogen Dominance"), there is an increased risk of breast cancer, blood clots, heart disease, stroke, gallbladder disease, endometrial cancer, and migraine.

Estrogen levels are in a constant state of flux, especially during women's childbearing years. In normal, healthy women, estrogen levels typically follow a 28-day cycle: they are lowest during menstruation, after which they rise rapidly near midcycle and decline just before ovulation (around days 12 through 15 of the cycle). During days 16 through 28, estrogen levels remain low, rising slightly again just before the onset of menstruation, while progesterone peaks around day 22, after which it declines rapidly before menstruation (see "Progesterone").

Therefore, in our Restorative Medicine Program, we restore estrogen levels by mimicking these fluctuations in estrogen and progesterone levels according to each woman's natural cycle.

Estrogen in Men

Along with a decline in testosterone levels with age in men (see "Testosterone"), many men also experience an increase in estrogen (estradiol) levels. This rise may result in an imbalance in the ratio between testosterone and estrogen, which can be accompanied by severely inhibited sexual desire and performance, an enlarged prostate, loss of muscle tone, fatigue, and increased body fat. High levels of estrogen in men also increase the risk of myocardial infarction, stroke, pulmonary embolism, rheumatoid arthritis, and peripheral artery disease. Elevated levels of estrogen in men can trick the brain into thinking that a sufficient amount of testosterone is being produced, which then results in a slowdown in the natural production of testosterone.

In men whose blood tests show high levels of estrogen and low testosterone, this situation could be the result of excess production of an enzyme called aromatase. As men age, they tend to produce larger quantities of this enzyme, which converts testosterone into estrogen. If we can inhibit the action of the aromatase enzyme, we can help keep estrogen levels in balance and thus a balanced estrogen/testosterone ratio. The aromatase inhibitor we use most often is zinc.

The Three Estrogens

In women, the three estrogens are present in the body in a ratio of approximately 60 to 80 percent estriol, and 10 to 20 percent each of estradiol and estrone. These are the guidelines we use when we prescribe bioidentical estrogen in our Restorative Medicine Program. Nature has a reason for these somewhat lopsided percentages:

- Estriol: We refer to this estrogen as the "safe" one because not only has it been found to help prevent breast cancer, it also is not associated with an increased risk of breast or ovarian cancer, as are estradiol and estrone.

- Estradiol: Estradiol has been found to have cancer-causing properties when it is in the body in an unbalanced state.

- Estrone: Like estradiol, estrone is a known carcinogen when it is in an unbalanced state.

The goal of our Restorative Medicine Program is to restore all three estrogens to optimal and balanced levels, in proper ratio with progesterone.

Taking Estrogen

We recommend a bioidentical form of estrogen gel called Triest®, which we recommend be formulated (by a compounding pharmacy) to consist of 90 percent estriol, 7 percent estradiol, and 3 percent estrone. We believe this formulation (or something very close to it, depending on the individual needs of the patient) is most beneficial for women, especially those older than thirty-five, because it provides levels of the three estrogens in safe, effective amounts.

Estrogen gel should be applied in the morning after bathing to areas that provide the best absorption, which include the vulva (best site), forearms, and neck. It is not necessary to change the application site every day.

Progesterone

Say "progesterone" and most people—especially women—immediately recognize it as a female hormone because it is so closely associated with pregnancy and menstruation. And they are partly right, as one of progesterone's most important functions is to cause the endometrium to secrete proteins during the second half of the menstrual cycle to prepare the uterus to accept an implanted fertilized egg. Progesterone is also associated with premenstrual syndrome (PMS), as low levels of this hormone are believed to be responsible for symptoms such as mood swings, water retention, breast tenderness, and headache, among other complaints. We believe high levels of cortisol can block progesterone from reaching its receptors. This leads to symptoms associated with the dominance of estrogen in relation to progesterone.

But progesterone is not solely a "female" hormone: it is found in both men and women, and in both sexes it works to balance and offset the powerful effects of another important hormone, estrogen. In fact, many of the complaints men and women have about aging—weight gain, insomnia, anxiety, depression, and migraine in women; weight gain, loss of sex drive, and prostate enlargement in men—are associated with an imbalance between estrogen and progesterone that is common in both men and women.

Progesterone, Progestogen, and Progestins

First we need to clear up any confusion about these three terms. Progesterone refers to the natural hormone that the body produces. In women it is manufactured primarily by the ovaries, although the adrenal glands make a contribution as well. In men, the adrenal glands and testes are the manufacturing sources. In our Restorative Medicine Program, we use natural micronized progesterone, which is created in the laboratory from soybeans or the Mexican wild yam (*Dioscorea villosa*) (see "Using Bioidenticall Progesterone", p.62). This form is an exact chemical duplicate of the progesterone that is produced by the human body.

The word "progestins" refers to non-bioidentical progesterone, like that found in birth control pills and conventional hormone replacement therapy, such as Provera (medroxyprogesterone). Finally, "progestogen" refers to any hormone product that affects the uterus in much the same way as natural progesterone. The term *progestogen* is an umbrella term that encompasses progesterone and non-bioidentical progestins (e.g., medroxyprogesterone).

Progesterone vs Progestins

The common progestins used in conventional hormone replacement therapy can be divided into those structurally related to progesterone (e.g., medroxyprogesterone acetate and nomegestrol) or testosterone (e.g., norethindrone and levonorgestrel). For example, medroxyprogesterone is a progestin that is an analog or "look alike" of progesterone. Although the chemical structure of medroxyprogesterone is close to that of progesterone, the slight differences can produce different responses from its natural counterpart.

Generally, progestins cause significantly more side effects than natural progesterone, and they are more severe. One reason for this is that **progestins can reduce a patient's level of progesterone.** Progestin use is associated with weight gain, headache, blood clots, acne, rashes, mood swings, and depression. Women who take bioidentical micronized progesterone, however, often report that these symptoms diminish or disappear.

Functions of Progesterone

Progesterone's many functions in the body include:

- Maintaining the uterine lining and preventing excess tissue buildup (which can result in endometriosis)

- Inhibiting overgrowth of breast tissue

- Increasing metabolism and promoting weight loss

- Balancing blood sugar (glucose) levels

- Acting as a natural diuretic

- Normalizing blood clotting

- Stimulating the production of new bone, which is important in preventing osteoporosis

- Enhancing the action of thyroid hormones

- Alleviating depression, reducing anxiety, and balancing mood

- Promoting normal sleep patterns

- Preventing cyclical migraines

- Restoring proper cell oxygen levels

- Improving libido

Decline in Progesterone/Estrogen Dominance

Women's progesterone levels typically begin to decline when they are in their early to mid thirties, and production declines much more rapidly than does estrogen production. This drop in progesterone levels causes the body to become estrogen dominant; that is, the natural ratio of estrogen to progesterone is out of balance. This can mean several things: estrogen levels are extremely high; estrogen levels are normal and progesterone is low, or estrogen is low and progesterone is extremely low.

Estrogen dominance causes various metabolic disturbances; the most common of which is weight gain because the body is unable to effectively burn stored fat for energy. Also, estrogen dominance compromises the body's ability to metabolize all types of calories or to distribute body weight evenly. Another indication of estrogen dominance is water retention and fat deposits on the hips, thighs, and abdomen.

While estrogen dominance is usually thought of as a "female" problem, excess estrogen in men can be detrimental as well. Along with the increased risk for cardiovascular and inflammatory diseases (see "Estrogen in Men"), elevated estrogen in men is associated with breast enlargement (gynecomastia), weight gain, prostate enlargement, and a decline in sexual function.

For more on the downside of progestins, see Chapter 2, "Why the Current Medicine Model Doesn't Work."

Using Bioidentical Progesterone

The form of bioidentical progesterone that we recommend is micronized progesterone USP. Micronized progesterone is available as a gel, which is the form we prefer, and also in capsule and tablet form. Micronization of progesterone is a process that creates minute crystals of the hormone, which are more readily and steadily absorbed through the skin or from the gastrointestinal tract. The USP stands for United States Pharmacopoeia, a national standard of purity for ingredients used in cosmetics and drugs. A micronized progesterone product that has USP on the label is your guarantee that the progesterone is a bioidentical form. Some progesterone gels contain wild yam extract only but have no USP progesterone. These products are not effective because the body cannot convert yam extracts into progesterone.

Micronized progesterone gel should have an oil/water emulsion base that also contains permeation enhancers, which increase the ability of the hormone to penetrate beyond the skin barrier and diffuse into the capillaries and then into the bloodstream. We recommend a micronized gel that delivers 50 mg/mL, which is available through compounding pharmacies. When we recommend progesterone gel for women, we emphasize that it should be applied in a cycle that mimics a healthy woman's normal menstrual cycle; that is, it should be applied in the morning. For some women and men, applying 25 percent of the daily dose at night more closely mimics their natural cycle, and this is something we help patients determine.

Testosterone

Testosterone is typically recognized as a male hormone, as it is responsible for the normal development of male sex and reproductive organs, and for development of secondary male sex traits (e.g., hair growth, muscle development, thickening of the vocal chord). Despite the very "macho" image most people have of this hormone, women also need testosterone, although their healthy levels are lower than those in men. In both men and women, it is important to maintain a balance of testosterone in relation to the other steroidal hormones.

In males, testosterone is manufactured by the Leydig cells of the testes, which are stimulated to produce the hormone by luteinizing hormone secreted by the pituitary gland. Small amounts are also made by steroids that are secreted by the adrenal cortex. In females, the ovaries make testosterone.

Testosterone exists in the bloodstream in two different forms: bound testosterone, which makes up the vast majority of the hormone; and free testosterone. Most of bound testosterone is attached chemically to a protein called "sex hormone binding globulin (SHBG). The rest of bound testosterone is bound to a different protein, albumin. Free testosterone is so-called because it is not bound to any proteins, which means it is the active form of testosterone and therefore ready and able to bind to receptor sites on cells.

The Life of Testosterone

In males, testosterone production rises rapidly when puberty begins and declines rapidly after age 50. Benefits of testosterone include:

- Promotes bone density and growth
- Helps in distribution of fat
- Maintains muscle mass
- Improves muscle strength
- Promotes sperm production

- Stimulates production of red blood cells

- Enhances sex drive

- Protects against chronic inflammatory disorders

Low testosterone levels in men can manifest as erectile dysfunction, low sex drive, depression, reduced muscle strength, memory loss, loss of muscle mass, increased breast size, weight gain (in the abdominal area), and irritability. Men also can experience a loss of bone density, which contributes to development of osteoporosis.

In women, the ovaries produce the majority of testosterone, and increased amounts are made during puberty, because testosterone is the precursor to estrogen. Women's testosterone levels peak when they are in their early twenties. Many women experience the effects of testosterone deficiency as they enter menopause, as estrogen, progesterone, and testosterone production declines dramatically. Low levels of testosterone in women are associated with little or no sex drive, especially among postmenopausal women, while supplementation can improve it.

Taking Testosterone

When we recommend testosterone supplements, our goal is not only to achieve an optimal level of the hormone, but also to place it in proper balance with other steroid hormones. For some people who have suboptimal testosterone levels, taking DHEA alone is enough to boost testosterone levels, because

DHEA can convert into testosterone. This approach is often possible in women. Males, however, do not experience the same level of conversion of DHEA to testosterone, so supplements are frequently recommended when indicated.

Testosterone levels fluctuate from hour to hour, but the highest levels occur in the early morning for both men and women. The optimal range for males is 650 to 827 ng/dL; for females, 60 to 76 ng/dL. When taking testosterone, patients can choose from capsules or tablets, injection, transdermal patch, or gel. We prefer gel because it is easy to use and dosing can be customized.

Cortisol

Cortisol is best known as a stress hormone because its level in the body rises when the body is subject to physical and/or emotional stress, including infection, injury, dieting, and strenuous activity. This hormone is synthesized from cholesterol and is produced by the adrenal glands, and more specifically, by the zona fasciculata section of the gland. It is the main glucocorticoid, and all glucocorticoids are essential in helping the body adapt to external stress and changes.

Cortisol production peaks in the early morning, typically about 7 AM, and is at its lowest point in the evening and during the early phase of sleep. Cortisol levels rise when the pituitary gland releases another hormone, adrenocorticotropic hormone (ACTH), which stimulates production. If your schedule is reversed (you work night shifts, for example, and sleep during the day), this natural rhythm may be reversed.

While chronically elevated levels of cortisol can be dangerous, low levels can be harmful as well. Therefore it is important to maintain a proper balance of all steroid hormones to help counterbalance any discord in cortisol levels and to strive to keep those levels at optimal as well.

Functions of Cortisol

Cortisol has far-reaching effects throughout the body. Some of its functions include:

- Regulating glucose levels

- Fighting inflammation

- Aiding in metabolism by breaking down carbohydrates, lipids, and proteins

- Stimulating protein catabolism to promote enzyme synthesis, energy production and tissue repair

- Maintaining blood pressure

Recent studies also show that cortisol may be involved in behavioral disorders, especially antisocial disorder (see Chapter 12, "Other Disorders"). Given that behavioral disorders are associated with major societal problems, including crime, abuse, disruption of family life, and difficulties in educating children who have these challenges, the need to find safe, effective treatments for such disorders is paramount. We believe restorative hormone therapy may be an answer.

DHEA and Cortisol

A special relationship exists between cortisol and DHEA, and establishing the proper ratio between these two hormones is critical in achieving and maintaining health and in ensuring a healthy response to stress. DHEA protects the body from the damage that high levels of cortisol can cause. The DHEA-to-cortisol ratio increases when people are calm or in low-stress situations, but it decreases during times of stress. Taking supplements of DHEA can increase the tolerance for stress, increases the DHEA:cortisol ratio, and protects the body against cortisol-induced cell damage.

Taking Cortisol

When cortisol is used as therapy, it is typically called hydrocortisone and is available in oral and injectable forms. It is used to relieve inflammation in people who have arthritis, asthma, severe allergies, and gastrointestinal disorders, such as colitis. It is also used to treat certain types of cancer. We rarely recommend cortisol in our Restorative Medicine Program, as taking DHEA supplements can restore the proper DHEA:cortisol ratio.

Side effects from hydrocortisone are not common, but if you overdose or do not balance your intake with an adequate amount of DHEA, you may experience weight gain, puffiness in the face and neck, and worsening of an underlying depression.

Melatonin

Melatonin is a hormone produced and secreted by the pineal gland, which is in the brain. The body makes melatonin by converting an amino acid called tryptophan into serotonin, a neurotransmitter and hormone that has the ability to control pain signals through regulation of blood vessel constriction in the brain. If the body does not have enough tryptophan and/or serotonin, it cannot make a sufficient amount of melatonin. Other factors that can lead to deficiencies of serotonin and melatonin include stress, chronic pain, and poor nutrition. Melatonin also has an association with cortisol: low levels of melatonin can cause cortisol secretion to get out of balance.

Melatonin is perhaps best known as a treatment for sleep problems and jet lag, but it also has antioxidant properties and can help strengthen the immune system. It also helps control the timing and release of female reproductive hormones and thus determines when menstruation begins, the frequency and duration of menstrual cycles, and when menopause occurs.

Melatonin and Circadian Rhythm

The human body has an internal biological clock that controls certain circadian functions (from Latin "circa diem" meaning *about a day* or *daily).* This "clock" is called the suprachiasmatic nucleus (SCN) and it's located in the hypothalamus. The SCN regulates the circadian rhythms of many different processes, including the sleep/wake cycle, hormone production, body temperature, blood pressure, and many others. Melatonin is usually associated with sleep disorders, as the production and release of melatonin are stimulated by darkness and suppressed by light. Blood levels of the hormone are highest prior to bedtime, an indication that melatonin is involved in the body's circadian rhythm and in the sleep/wake cycle.

Here's how it works. When light enters the eyes, it activates cells in the retina, which sends signals along the optic nerve to the SCN, which produces other signals. Some of the signals travel to the pineal gland, announcing that light is present, which causes the gland to shut down production of melatonin. Thus melatonin levels stay low during daylight, but as night approaches, the pineal gland receives signals that light is absent.

Once light is gone, melatonin production kicks into gear. As melatonin levels increase, the individual becomes drowsy. Melatonin levels usually peak just before midnight, then gradually decline over the next few hours. As they decline the body gradually wakes up, and the entire cycle begins again.

Taking Melatonin

Melatonin supplements are available in a wide range of dosages. In our Restorative Medicine Program, we often recommend taking melatonin along with kava root extract and Vitamin B6, as these complement each other in the treatment of many conditions. Most patients who take melatonin can stop the hormone after two to three months, as their pineal circadian cycle is restored. If sleep problems then return, taking melatonin a few days per month usually restores balance and eliminates symptoms. Side effects are rare and usually occur when individuals take too large of a dose. In such cases morning grogginess, dizziness, and irritability may result.

Nutrients and Other Natural Supplements

We typically recommend various vitamins, minerals, herbs, or other natural supplements as part of our Restorative Medicine Program. The items are chosen based on each patient's unique needs. In most cases, patients take the recommended supplements only until they have achieved hormonal balance and/or their symptoms have been resolved.

The following list includes those nutrients and supplements that we often recommend to our patients. You will have an opportunity to see when and how they are used throughout the second part of this book, where we explain how our Restorative Medicine Program can be implemented for a wide variety of conditions.

Magnesium

Magnesium is the fourth most abundant mineral in the human body, and it is a player in more than three hundred biochemical reactions. This information, along with the fact that about 20 percent of adults do not consume even 50 percent of the recommended amount (250-500 mg), highlights the importance of making sure everyone gets enough of this mineral.

Our Restorative Medicine Program recommends magnesium in the form of magnesium citrate (which is the form best absorbed by the body) and is recommended to nearly all patients, because it addresses so many of the symptoms that accompany conditions caused by hormone imbalance. Magnesium is important in relieving migraine and symptoms of premenstrual syndrome, and in regulating the central nervous system. Magnesium, along with Vitamin B6, is necessary for the production of serotonin, which is a mood-enhancing chemical and a precursor of the hormone melatonin. A balanced ratio of magnesium to calcium is critical not only for bone health, but for blood pressure, sleep, migraine, and fatigue.

Probiotics

Probiotics are beneficial, live bacteria that can be taken in supplement form to help restore the balance of bacterial flora in the intestinal tract. As you will learn, a healthy intestinal tract is a critical necessity for overall health and thus a crucial part of our Restorative Medicine Program. Probiotics are recommended to most all our patients, and typically continued for several months, or until hormonal balance is achieved. Some patients then take probiotics occasionally, as needed, to address any gastrointestinal issues that may arise, such as constipation, diarrhea, or gas. Probiotics also help enhance absorption of nutrients into the bloodstream, promote function of the intestinal cells, and improve general health. You can learn more about probiotics in Chapter 12.

Kava Root Extract

Derived from the root of *Piper methysticum,* kava root extract has a calming effect, which is attributed to plant components called kavalactones. That makes kava root extract an ideal supplement to promote sleep and tranquility, and to relax deep muscles. We recommend it as part of a proprietary formula along with melatonin and vitamin B6, but patients can also purchase each of the supplements separately.

Kava extracts have been used extensively for many years by people throughout the world by peoples in many cultures. In 2002, one report by a German research team suggested that use of kava may cause liver damage. The European Union and Canada quickly banned the herb, but it is still marketed and used in the United States, albeit with a warning label about possible liver damage.

We want to assure you that based on our evaluation and experience, the results of this one Germany study are not valid. One reason is that most of the people in the study who had side effects were using more than ten times the recommended daily dose of kava: 100 to 500 mg is typical, while study subjects were using 1,000 to 4,000 mg. Another reason is that many of the people who had liver damage also consumed alcohol regularly. Yet another point is that most of the people who had liver damage were also taking at least one other prescription medication, which increases the chances of liver problems.

The bottom line is that our experience shows that taking kava in clinically tested doses is very safe. Several studies subsequent to the one released in 2002, including a meta-analysis of eleven trials, show that kava extract is safe.

Saw Palmetto

Saw palmetto is an herb (*Serenoa repens)* that is indigenous to the United States. It has several uses, but it's most important role in our Restorative Medicine Program is to block conversion of testosterone to DHT, the metabolite of testosterone that stimulates growth of the prostate gland and also causes hair loss. More specifically, saw palmetto inhibits the activity of the enzyme 5-alpha-reductase, which converts testosterone to DHT. We are using saw palmetto for most females after age 40 because it can prevent development or reduce such problems as hair loss, facial hair, and acne.

The typical dose of saw palmetto that we recommend is 160 mg once daily. Usually, the use of saw palmetto supplements is associated with very few side effects. In our clinical work, we did not see any.

Zinc

This mineral is often recommended to inhibit aromatase, an enzyme that is involved in the conversion of testosterone into estrogen. In women, zinc can be helpful in achieving and maintaining an estrogen-progesterone balance. In men, zinc is typically used along with saw palmetto for prostate enlargement and erectile dysfunction. The typical dose of zinc can range from 15 to 90 mg daily.

Human Growth Hormone

Human growth hormone (HGH) is manufactured in the pituitary gland. It reaches peak levels around puberty and then begins to decline around age 40. HGH supplements have been shown to increase muscle mass and reduce the amount of fat in healthy older adults. It has an indirect affect on the metabolism of cholesterol, as it helps to control the lipase that regulates a conversion of triglycerides to free fatty acids. Low levels of HGH can result in high total cholesterol, heart disease, low bone density, and disturbances in psychological function.

Part II

Diseases
and Medical Conditions

Chapter 4

THE HEART OF THE MATTER: CARDIOVASCULAR DISEASE

Vicky found it hard to believe her doctor when he told her that she was at high risk for heart disease. The forty-five-year-old attorney prided herself on eating well and exercising whenever she could. She was not overweight and did not smoke, and enjoyed a glass fr wine or two at least several times a week. But Vicky's latest physical revealed high blood pressure, high cholesterol, and high homocysteine levels, all strong risk factors for coronary heart disease. She also worked more than 70 hours a week, and her doctor was concerned about her stress level as well. For the first time in her life, Vicky felt uneasy about her future, a feeling she had never entertained before now. She had a teenage daughter, a loving husband, and a great job, and she didn't want to do anything to jeopardize any of it.

Coronary Heart Disease

Coronary heart disease (CHD) is the most common type of heart disease and the number one cause of mortality and morbidity in the developed world for both women and men. According to the Centers for Disease Control and Prevention and the National Center for Health Statistics, nearly 500,000 people die from coronary heart disease per year, which representes about 71 percent of all heart disease deaths. Approximately two-thirds of people who die of CHD are older than 55; however, that leaves a significant number of younger men and women who die of the disease each year.

The disease develops when the walls of the coronary arteries, which wrap around the heart and provide it with oxygen and nutrients, become narrowed and inflexible due to an accumulation of fatty deposits called plaque. Over time the buildup of plaque continues to narrow the coronary arteries, blood flow to the heart muscle declines, and the heart is starved of nutrients and oxygen. Diagnosis: coronary heart disease.

Eventually CHD can weaken the heart muscle and promote the development of congestive heart failure, a condition in which the heart can no longer effectively pump blood to the rest of the body.

A Little History

In 1856, Rudolph Virchow proposed that the accumulation of lipids (e.g., cholesterol, triglycerides) in the arteries caused atherosclerosis, which in itself is a primary cause of coronary heart disease. Nearly 100 years later, John Gofman (1950) hypothesized that cholesterol in the bloodstream was the main cause of CHD. The year 1953 saw publication of the paper that discussed how cholesterol and saturated fats were the cause of heart disease. Investigators found that people who died of heart disease often had high levels of cholesterol in their blood, and many studies confirmed that elevated cholesterol was associated with an increased risk of atherosclerosis. What most experts and the public need to note, however, is the key word—"associated." A big question, you see, is this: Did the patients die from high cholesterol, or was their cholesterol level high because of serious physiologic dysfunctions, and the patients actually died from those malfunctions?

We know from previous chapters that cholesterol is important in the creation of hormones. Now let's look at cholesterol from a different angle: its role in two somewhat related conditions, hypercholesterolemia (high cholesterol) and coronary heart disease.

Women and Coronary Heart Disease

Many people think of coronary heart disease as a "male" problem. In fact, 38 percent of women in the United States die within one year of suffering a heart attack, compared with 25 percent of men. Women tend to develop CHD later in life than men do, which means their greatest risk years are postmenopause. This is when their levels of ovarian hormones decline dramatically. However, at least one third of the people who die of CHD are younger than 55 years. So the risk, while greater in older people, is still very real in younger individuals.

The risk factors for CHD include those over which people have no control--age, family history, gender, and ethnicity— but also those that can be modified through lifestyle changes, such as high cholesterol, high homocysteine, high blood pressure, diabetes, high C-reactive protein, overweight or obesity, smoking, lack of physical activity, and high stress. Another factor that can be modified is hormone levels.

Hormones and Heart Disease

Given that women's risk of CHD increases greatly after menopause, it appears that female hormones provide some protection against heart disease. Women became alarmed; however, when the Women's Health Initiative (WHI) did not support the idea that conventional hormone replacement therapy offered protection from CHD.

We believe that trials such as the WHI did not uncover a cardioprotective effect of female hormones for several critical reasons:

- Researchers did not use hormones that were bioidentical to those produced by the human body

- Researchers used only one or two hormones (most often estrogen or estrogen/progestin) rather than the five essential steroid hormones.

- The dosing strategy was not individualized, but instead was a one-size-fits-all approach

- The hormones were not given in a manner that mimics a woman's normal menstrual cycle

- The hormones were given in oral form. Hormones that are taken orally are metabolized and modified by the liver in ways that do not allow the body to utilize them the way that yields the intended effect.

We have learned much about the effect of estrogen on the cardiovascular system in recent years. Until just a few years ago, the consensus was that the lower incidence of CHD in women before menopause was due to the protective effect estrogen had on the coronary arteries because it regulated cholesterol. However, since then the data show that estrogen can inhibit damage to blood vessels and the development of atherosclerosis. Some evidence also exists that DHEA supplementation may prevent cardiovascular problems in women, mainly because of this hormone's estrogenic effect. Testosterone has also been shown to inhibit the formation of plaque.

Our experience using bioidentical hormones has shown that, unlike non-bioidentical hormones, those that are identical to the ones produced by the human body help bring the body back into balance and eliminate the signs and symptoms resulting from hormone imbalance. We therefore suggest that hormone restorative therapy using hormones bioidentical to humans significantly decreases several risk factors for CHD. Paula's case is a good example.

Paula's Story

Paula is a white, 50-year-old former high school teacher who came to see us shortly after she retired early from her career due to increasing health problems. At the time of her first visit, her weight was good for her height (125 lb and 5' 4"). Her signs and symptoms included poorly controlled (with medication) high blood pressure (150/90 mmHg), migraine, high cholesterol (241 mg/dL), depression, severe anxiety, irritability, fatigue, poor libido, low sex drive, genital herpes, sleep problems, poor short-term memory, weight gain, arthritis, and an irregular menstrual cycle. She told us that she had suffered with most of these problems for the last 10 to 15 years, but that they had gotten increasingly worse.

We talked to Paula about her risk factors for CHD, which included hypertension, high cholesterol, depression, and anxiety, and how a broad approach to treatment could dramatically reduce her chances of developing the disease. She agreed to try our Restorative Medicine Program.

"I was so relieved that someone felt they could actually help me," she said. "I had been suffering so long with so many symptoms, and now with the increased risk of heart problems, I didn't want to take any chances. I have dreamed of going back to work some day, and now I have some hope that it may happen."

During Paula's first visit she revealed that she was taking three medications for high blood pressure (triametere/hydrochlorothiazide, Procardia XL®, and Nifedical XL®), Premphase (for vaginal dryness and hot flashes), Zoloft ® (depression), Butisol Sodium® and Ambien® (for sleeping disorder), and Zovirax® and Valtrex® (genital herpes). The results of her initial blood tests showed significantly imbalanced basic steroid hormone levels, including extremely high estrogen and low levels of the other four steroid hormones (see chart).

Hormone	Reference Range	Paula
DHEA-S	65-380 ug/dL	66 ug/dL
Pregnenolone	10-230 ng/dL	50 ng/dL
Total Estrogen	61-437 pg/mL	643 pg/mL
Progesterone:	0.2-28 ng/mL	0.7 ng/mL
Total Testosterone	14-76 ng/dL	29 ng/dL

Paula's initial Program was designed to restore hormonal balance. Her daily regimen of bioidentical hormones included the following. All doses were taken in the morning unless noted otherwise:

- Pregnenolone: 100 mg
- DHEA: 50 mg

- Triest gel (containing a 90:7:3 ratio of estriol, estradiol, and estrone): 0.6 ml on days 1-10 following menses, and 0.4 ml until menses begin

- Micronized progesterone gel (50 mg/ml): 0.6 ml on days 1-10 after menses, 0.8 ml until menses begins

- Micronized testosterone gel (50 mg/ml): 0.1 ml daily

We also added other supplements to address some of her other symptoms:

- Omega-3 fatty acids, 1,000 mg (for heart health and to enhance memory)

- Proprietary high potency vitamin/mineral/ phytonutrient formula, 3 tablets taken three times daily

- Glucosamine sulfate, 2,000 mg (for relief of arthritis symptoms)

- Phosphatidylserine, 200 mg (to enhance memory)

- Proprietary formula that contains green foods, plant fibers, bioflavonoids, herbal extracts, and probiotics (3.5 billion Lactobacillus group, 1.0 billion Bifidobacterium group, and 0.5 billion Streptococcus thermophilus), one scoop in the morning (for gastrointestinal complaints)

Three days after starting the Program, Paula stopped taking Premphase. During the first month of treatment, her blood pressure improved from 150/90 to 130/90 mmHg, her migraines decreased in frequency and severity, and her arthritis pain disappeared.

"I can't tell you how great it was to be free of joint pain and to have less migraine pain," said Paula. "And knowing that my blood pressure was going down was a great relief as well. I felt like I was finally making progress."

At that time we increased her DHEA supplement to 100 mg in the morning and 50 mg at noon, and we added 0.2 ml of progesterone and 420 mg of magnesium citrate to be taken one hour before bedtime (for better sleep and blood pressure control).

During the next three months Paula reported that her depression and anxiety had improved so much she felt ready to gradually stop Zoloft and Butisol sodium, which she did under medical supervision. By this time she was taking only one anti-hypertensive medication (Procardia XL), and because her sleep had improved significantly, she also stopped the Ambien.

"After only three months on the Program, I felt like a new person," said Paula. "I suddenly had energy, and so I started to walk several times a week and take an aerobics class twice a week. I hadn't had the energy to do any kind of exercise for years!"

At the three-month mark in the Program we added 0.5 IU human growth hormone taken daily six days per week, and androstenedione, 50 mg taken 30 minutes before exercise. We also reduced DHEA to 50 mg daily and increased pregnenolone to 200 mg in the morning.

At Paula's one-year anniversary of treatment, she had gone 12-months without an episode of genital herpes, so she stopped her medication for that disease. She also had not experienced a migraine for nearly a year, and said her memory problems had disappeared as well. She has fulfilled her dream of returning to the classroom and now enjoys a healthy lifestyle, regular exercise, and a balanced diet, while remaining on restorative hormones and nutritional supplements.

Bernadette's Story

When Bernadette first came to see us, this 56-year-old white grandmother of two had a history of chronic fatigue syndrome, obesity (232 lbs at 4' 10"), severe shortness of breath, high blood pressure (168/86 mmHg), type 2 diabetes, depression, anxiety, panic attacks, insomnia, arthritis, overall body aches, hot flashes, vaginal dryness, no sexual desire, vaginal yeast infections, short-term memory problems, and an admitted "addiction" to chocolate.

Most of Bernadette's symptoms had begun when she was 44 years old and was going through a divorce. At that time she weighed 118 pounds. Her prior medical history had included a complete hysterectomy at age 30 because of fibroids. After we reviewed her personal and family medical history, we talked to her about her risk factors for CHD, which included obesity, shortness of breath, high blood pressure, type II diabetes, depression, anxiety, and panic attacks. After discussing our

Restorative Medicine Program with her, she agreed to undergo laboratory testing.

"I guess I already knew I was in danger of heart problems," said Bernadette. "I was so overweight and always out of breath. I had no energy to exercise and no will to do so. But I wanted to get better so I could enjoy my grandchildren, and I had another one on the way. They were my motivation."

Bernadette gave us a list of the medications she was taking when we first saw her: Glucophage® and glyburide (diabetes), Zestril® and hydrochlorothiazide (blood pressure), Wellbutrin® (depression), Premarin® (hot flashes, sexual problems), Tylenol® (pain), various vitamins and minerals, and two weight-loss supplements.

Her blood test results revealed dramatically high estrogen levels and low levels of the other steroid hormones (see chart).

Hormone	Reference Range	Bernadette
DHEA-S	65-380 ug/dL	35 ug/dL
Pregnenolone	10-230 ng/dL	<10 ng/dL
Total Estrogen	61-437 pg/mL	699 pg/mL
Progesterone:	0.2-28 ng/mL	0.2 ng/mL
Total Testosterone	14-76 ng/dL	16 ng/dL

Given the lab results, we started Bernadette on the following program. All doses were taken in the morning unless noted otherwise:

- Pregnenolone: 200 mg

- DHEA: 100 mg

- Triest gel: 1 ml on days 1-14, 0.8 ml on days 15-25, and 0.4 ml on the last five to six days of each month

- Micronized progesterone gel (50 mg/ml): 0.8 ml on days 1-14, 1 ml on days 15-25, and 0.6 ml on the last five to six days of each month

- Micronized testosterone gel (50 mg/ml): 0.2 ml every day

- Phosphatidylserine: 200 mg (to enhance memory)

- Proprietary blend of 3 mg melatonin, 250 mg kava root extract, and 10 mg Vitamin B6 in a capsule, one capsule at bedtime (for sleep problems)

- Chromium: 400 mcg twice daily (for diabetes)

Two days after starting treatment, Bernadette stopped taking Premarin. We suggested she reduce her intake of carbohydrates and begin an exercise program, which she did by starting a walking program. When she came in for her one-month follow-up visit, she was in good spirits.

"I feel so much better already," she said. "I've lost 10 pounds, and I have so much energy, I can't believe it. Since I feel so good, I stopped taking my antidepressant and I don't need the Tylenol any more either. My goal is to stop taking all these drugs if possible and to lose more weight."

At the one-month mark we added the following to her Program:

- Glucosamine sulfate, 2,250 mg (for arthritis symptoms)

- Androstenedione, 50 mg taken 30 minutes before exercise (to assist with physical activity)

- Progesterone, 0.2 mg, and magnesium citrate, 420 mg, taken one hour before bedtime

After four months on the Program, Bernadette had lost an additional 28 pounds, her blood pressure was 120/80 mmHg, and her blood glucose was stable. At this point we added the following supplements:

- Conjugated linoleic acid (CLA), 8 grams before breakfast (to assist with weight loss)

- Chitosan, two capsules before lunch and two before dinner (to assist with weight loss)

- Hydroxycitric acid (HCA), 1,000 mg capsule taken three times daily before meals (to assist with weight loss)

- B-complex, one tablet daily

- Omega-3 fatty acids, 3,000 mg taken twice daily

- A one-month parasite-cleansing program (to assist with weight loss and absorption of nutrients)

One year after starting the Program, Bernadette had reached her goal of stopping her medications: her blood pressure and glucose levels were stable without medication. She had also significantly reduced her risk of CHD. Bernadette continued to gradually lose weight and had lots of energy for her three grandchildren.

Hormones and the Male Heart

In case you think we forgot to talk about men and heart disease, let us reassure you that restorative hormone therapy is also recommended for males. Testosterone is a key factor in the health of the heart. This fact ties in nicely with another: that the heart has more testosterone receptors than any other organ in the body. Testosterone can lower LDL cholesterol and triglyceride levels; low amounts of the hormone can have an opposite, negative effect. Studies show, for example, that hypotestosteronemia (low testosterone levels) is associated with acute myocardial infarction and coronary artery disease. One-quarter of men with coronary heart disease have clinically deficient levels of testosterone. When we introduce another fact—that testosterone levels decline with age, and in men this is associated with andropause—you have the makings of an increased risk for heart problems.

As you already know, it is critical to balance all the hormones we have discussed in this book, and it is no different when it comes to males and heart disease. In men, we are especially interested in the balance between testosterone and estradiol. Studies show that low testosterone and high estradiol levels are associated with cardiovascular disease in men. In women, however, estrogen (bioidentical to that produced by the body when referring to supplements) offers protection against heart disease.

It's also been shown that DHEA protects men against heart disease. Unlike testosterone levels, which typically decline very gradually over the years, DHEA levels drop dramatically. By age 40, men have only about 50 percent the DHEA they had in their twenties. Thus men in their fifties and sixties tend to have very low levels of DHEA, in need of restoration. When it comes to the heart, DHEA supplementation helps reduce death from coronary heart disease and slows the progression of atherosclerosis.

Thus restoration of both testosterone and DHEA levels in men can result in significant protection against coronary heart disease, congestive heart failure, and other cardiovascular events.

Congestive Heart Failure

Approximately 5 million Americans suffer from congestive heart failure (CHF), in which the heart cannot pump enough oxygen-rich blood to the body to meet its needs. This often fatal disease—20 percent of patients die within one year of diagnosis and 50 percent die within five years—can be caused by diseases that weaken the heart muscles (e.g., heart attack, myocarditis), stiffen the heart muscles (e.g. hemochromatosis, amyloidosis; commonly caused by chronic high blood pressure), or those that increase the demand for oxygen beyond the ability of the heart to deliver it (e.g., hyperthyroidism). Other conditions that may lead to CHF include congenital heart disease, diabetes, anemia, obstructive sleep apnea, lupus, rheumatoid arthritis, hyperthyroidism, alcoholism, and abuse of drugs such as cocaine and amphetamines.

It is commonly recognized that advancing age is the most powerful risk factor for congestive heart failure, but the majority of conventional health-care providers do not completely accept what we have come to believe: that low testosterone production may play a significant role in this disease. In addition, studies also show that patients with CHF often have low levels of DHEA, estrogen, and insulin-like growth factor 1 (IGF-1) as well.

The impact of congestive heart failure reaches beyond the heart to other organs throughout the body. Congestion in and around the lungs, for example, is a very common complication in people who have congestive heart failure, as is swelling of the ankles and lower legs. The kidneys, vascular system, and brain also can be affected.

Conventional Treatment

The conventional treatment approach to CHF includes administration of drugs that address high blood pressure, arrhythmia, anemia, thyroid dysfunction, coronary artery disease, and valvular abnormalities. These drugs typically include diuretics (reduce accumulated fluids), angiotensin-converting enzyme (ACE) inhibitors (improves blood flow), beta-blockers (slow heart rate), digoxin (increases the ability of the heart to contract), and vasodilators (improve blood flow). In some cases, invasive procedures may be used, including balloon angioplasty, coronary stenting, coronary artery bypass surgery, heart valve surgery, insertion of a pacemaker, and heart transplantation.

Complementary Treatment Strategy

Contrary to the conventional treatment approach, we propose a method that focuses on lifestyle modifications and natural remedies, an approach that can be very effective if patients are aggressive and dedicated to the plan. A complementary approach includes:

- Maintaining a healthy weight, which reduces unnecessary stress on the heart

- Following healthy dietary guidelines, including restricted salt intake, use of monounsaturated oils, and consuming foods high in fiber (including fruits, vegetables, and whole grains) and essential fatty acids

- Use of hormone restoration therapy. We discuss this in more detail below.

- Supplementing with a variety of vitamins, minerals, herbs, and other natural substances. Most patients with CHF symptoms are malnourished, and so supplementation is a critical part of the restoration process. We discuss these supplements in more detail below.

- Avoiding excessive use of alcohol. Men should limit consumption to no more than two drinks daily; women, one daily.

Natural Supplements for CHF

- **Coenzyme Q10** is produced by the body and is necessary for the basic functioning of all cells. It plays an important role in improving heart muscle function and has been shown to improve CHF symptoms.

- **Taurine** is an amino acid found in very high concentrations in healthy heart tissue, and low concentrations in heart muscle are associated with heart failure. Double-blind studies show that supplementation with taurine reduces the signs and symptoms of CHF and also minimizes many of the side effects of ACE inhibitors, which are the main drugs used in the treatment of CHF.

- **Hawthorn** and other herbs in the hawthorn family have long been used to treat cardiovascular diseases. Numerous studies show that hawthorn helps improve heart function and exercise tolerance. The recommended daily dose ranges from 160 to 900 mg.

- **Magnesium** supplements have been effective in treating fast, irregular heart beat and other life-threatening conditions associated with CHF.

- **Alpha-lipoic acid** helps reduce the damage caused by free radicals (oxidative stress), which is a major factor in the development and progression of CHF.

- **Vitamins**, including Vitamin C (supplies energy for cell metabolism), Vitamin E (important because of its antioxidant properties), and B-complex (promotes heart muscle health, physical endurance, and improved heart function).

- **L-arginine** is an amino acid that plays many roles in the body. It is necessary to create urea, a waste product that is needed for ammonia to be eliminated from the body. It is also needed to make creatine (see below). For heart health, arginine changes into nitric oxide, which causes blood vessels to relax and thus can improve chest pain, atherosclerosis, coronary artery disease, intermittent claudication, and peripheral vascular disease.

- **Creatine** is naturally synthesized in the body from amino acids mainly in the kidney and liver. Approximately 95 percent of the body's total creatine is located in skeletal muscle. Creatine is involved in energy production and cardiac function.

- **Fish oil** is a rich source of the omega-3 fatty acids eicosapentaenoic acid (EPA) and docosahexaenoic acid (DHA), which has been shown to reduce the risk of heart disease.

Restorative hormone therapy is also a key component of treatment for CHF. People with CHF often have elevated levels of cortisol and low levels of testosterone and DHEA, as well as low amounts of estrogen and IGF-1. Overall, however, our studies have shown that it is critical to restore all the steroid hormones to optimal levels to effectively treat CHF. Although no supplement or dietary plan can cure congestive heart failure, we find that restoring hormone balance, with the addition of specific natural supplements, can provide cardiovascular protection, improve cardiac function, and enhance the lives of people with this often fatal disease.

Chapter 5

CHOLESTEROL: THE HIGHS, THE LOWS

It seems like cholesterol is always in the news: we hear how bad it is, which foods we need to avoid because they are high in cholesterol, and which foods to eat to help bring levels down. Perhaps most frightening of all, however, is the message from the pharmaceutical and medical communities about how more people "need" to take statin drugs to control the growing epidemic of high cholesterol.

There is no denying that hypercholesterolemia (high cholesterol) is a major risk factor for cardiovascular disease, including coronary heart disease, stroke, and myocardial infarction. The World Health Organization estimates that nearly 20 percent of all strokes and more than 50 percent of all heart attacks can be linked to high cholesterol.

In this chapter we acknowledge the seriousness of cholesterol, but we also turn conventional "wisdom" on its head by stating that high cholesterol is not caused by eating too much high-cholesterol food or by a liver that is producing high amounts of the fat: **the cause of excess cholesterol is a multi-hormone deficiency.**

How can we make that statement? You will learn more about it in this chapter. Just let us say this as an opener: because cholesterol is the precursor to pregnenolone, DHEA, cortisol, testosterone, progesterone, and estrogens, when the body becomes deficient in these hormones, as eventually happens in most people, the body responds by overproducing cholesterol in an attempt to restore a healthy hormone balance.

The result? High cholesterol.

Cholesterol: The Pros and Cons

Cholesterol is a peculiar molecule. Although it is often called a lipid, a steroid, or a fat, it does not exactly fit the definitions of these agents. It is composed of four hydrocarbon rings, three of which are six-carbon rings, and one of which is a five-carbon ring, therefore it definitely is not a fat. Cholesterol is also considered a sterol (a combination steroid and alcohol), but it doesn't behave like alcohol.

Cholesterol presents in the blood and in all the body's cells. It has gotten a bad name because it is associated with hardening of the arteries (atherosclerosis) and heart disease, and it is true that this fatty substance can contribute to these serious medical conditions. But cholesterol has a good side as well, and when it is present in the body in a balanced way, it offers many benefits. For example:

- Cholesterol is the main component in cell membranes; without it, cell integrity could not be maintained and you could not exist.

- If you don't have enough cholesterol, your body won't produce enough sex hormones, and Vitamin D-3. As you learned in Chapter 3, cholesterol is the precursor for a cascade of critical hormones, including sex hormones.

Scores of studies have shown that cholesterol is not only an important substance to watch, but that **the right amount in the body** is critical. That is, attempts to bring cholesterol levels down **too low** as well as allowing cholesterol levels to remain **too high** are both harbingers of health problems. Here are just a few of the findings scientists have discovered about cholesterol:

- Blood cholesterol levels rise with each ten-year period until age 70, when they stabilize and then decline. By age 80, there is typically a significant drop in cholesterol levels. Therefore, while the mean cholesterol level for people age 20 to 29 is 188 mg/dL, it rises steadily to a mean of 237 mg/dL for people age 60 to 69, and then declines to about 218 mg/dL in people in their eighties.

- The body naturally produces more cholesterol when physical demands are placed on it, such as pregnancy, stress, starvation, exercise, childhood growth, and when the immune system is responding to injury, disease, or tissue repair. This is the body's natural defense against the damage of such stress.

• Total cholesterol levels are decreased in women who are at great risk of miscarriage.

• Up to 70% of patients with coronary heart disease or myocardial infarction (heart attack) have normal total cholesterol levels.

• People with psychiatric disorders (depression, suicidal ideation, impulsive aggressive behavior, schizophrenia, etc) and abuse issues (alcohol, heroin and other illicit drugs) often have low total cholesterol.

• Studies show an association between low total cholesterol and higher mortality rates from cancer, liver disease, and respiratory disorders.

• There is evidence that patients with low total cholesterol have the highest rates of death from CHD whereas those with elevated total cholesterol levels seem to have a lower risk.

Cholesterol, Lipoproteins, and Triglycerides

Cholesterol does not dissolve in the blood and so it must be transported to and from the cells via carriers called lipoproteins. Low-density lipoproteins (LDL) and high-density lipoproteins (HDL) are two of the main types. According to the traditional point of view, LDL is also called "bad cholesterol" (even though "LDL" is not "cholesterol"), because LDL particles are involved in the formation of plaques in the walls of the arteries and increase the risk of heart attack and stroke. HDL is "good cholesterol" (even though "HDL" is not "cholesterol") because it helps to remove cholesterol from the arterial walls. HDL aacts as a cholesterol mop, scavenging loose cholesterol and transporting it back to the liver.

Triglycerides are important "players" in heart disease. High levels of triglycerides increase the risk of cardiovascular problems.

When determining a person's risk for high cholesterol and the many complications that it can cause, clinicians look at reference figures established by the American Heart Association. In the United States and some other countries, cholesterol is measured in milligrams (mg) of cholesterol per deciliter (dL) of blood. Here's a breakdown of the figures:

Total Cholesterol	
< 200 mg/dL	Desirable
201-239 mg/dL	Borderline High
> 240 mg/dL	High

Low-Density Lipoprotein	
< 70 mg/dL	Optimal for people at very high risk of heart disease
< 100 mg/dL	Optimal for people at risk of heart disease
100-129 mg/dL	Near Optimal
130-159 mg/dL	Borderline High
160-189 mg/dL	High
> 240 mg/dL	Very High

High-Density Lipoprotein	
< 40 mg/dL (men)	Poor: higher risk for heart disease
< 40 mg/dL (women)	Poor: higher risk for heart disease
40-50 mg/dL (men)	Better: average risk for heart disease
50-60 mg/dL (women)	Better: average risk for heart disease
> 60 mg/dL	Best

Triglycerides	
< 150 mg/dL	Normal
150-199 mg/dL	Borderline High
200-499 mg/dL	High
> 500 mg/dL	Very High

According to the American Heart Association, an estimated 106.7 million adults in the United States have total blood cholesterol levels of 200 mg/dL and higher. Of these, 37.2 million have levels of 240 mg/dL or greater. How can these millions of people reduce their cholesterol levels safely and effectively? Those who practice conventional medicine typically recommend reducing intake of high-cholesterol foods (e.g., eggs, liver, beef, chicken, shrimp, and butter) and take drugs, specifically statins, which are associated with serious side effects. Yet these recommendations do not address the underlying reason why the body is overproducing cholesterol. Nor do they correct hormone deficiencies or restore hormonal balance in the body.

Hormone Restoration for High Cholesterol

Our research and clinical experience have lead us to hypothesize that high cholesterol (hypercholesterolemia) is the body's response to an age-related decline in steroidal hormones and hormone imbalance, and that it is characterized by a malfunction of the enzyme system, which results in a reduced ability to produce steroid hormones even though there is an excess of cholesterol.

One test of our hypothesis was conducted between July 1997 and April 2003, during which we treated 41 patients who had high cholesterol. All the patients (ages 25 to 81 years) received bioidentical hormones based on their individual hormone test results, and the hormones were administered in ratios with dose schedules that simulated natural hormone production cycles. The hormones given included oral pregnenolone, DHEA capsules, and topical triestrogen (estradiol, estrone, and estriol), progesterone, and testosterone gels.

In our study, all patients experienced an improvement in cholesterol levels. Mean serum total cholesterol levels dropped by 25.6 percent (from 254.6 mg/dL before the study to 188.8 mg/dL after treatment). Low-density lipoprotein levels decreased by 23.9 percent (from 158.2 mg/dL before treatment to 120.4 mg/dL after treatment). High-density lipoprotein levels decreased from 59.7 mg/dL to 48.0 mg/dL (a 19.6% decline).

High-Density Lipoprotein Levels

In most studies that attempt to reduce cholesterol levels, HDL levels usually rise rather than fall. In our study, HDL levels decreased to a level in the "better/poor" range. We believe that a declining HDL level is a positive sign that hormonal therapy has worked, and here's why: when we normalize total cholesterol, there is no longer a need for the body to produce extra HDL that serves as a carrier, because there is nothing to transport back to the liver. That is, an equilibrium has been reached between total cholesterol, LDL, and HDL, and the need for higher HDL levels disappears.

Low-Density Lipoprotein Levels

Our study also showed that LDL levels decreased on average from 158.2 mg/dL to 120.4 mg/dL, which is a significant decline. We must remember that restoring thyroid hormone levels may also help to normalize or reduce LDL. Thyroid hormone deficiency is not uncommon as people age, and low thyroid hormone levels cause elevated total cholesterol and LDL. Therefore, thyroid hormone levels should be checked and restoration may be part of hormone therapy for some individuals.

Raymond's Story

The impact of restorative hormone therapy on high cholesterol can perhaps be most dramatically demonstrated by telling Raymond's story. Raymond has familial hypercholesterolemia, an inherited condition in which the body is unable to remove low-density lipoprotein cholesterol from the bloodstream. The result is consistently high levels of LDL and total cholesterol. In most cases, individuals inherit the abnormal gene for the disease from one parent and typically have total cholesterol levels greater than 300 mg/dL, LDL levels greater than 200 mg/dL, and high triglycerides. In rare cases, children inherit the gene from both parents, and these people may have cholesterol levels that exceed 600 mg/dL.

Overall, people who have a family history of high cholesterol are at increased risk for heart attacks and heart disease.

Raymond, a 38-year-old insurance agent (5'11", weight 225 lbs), had a cholesterol level greater than 500 mg/dL and a triglyceride level greater than 1,500 mg/dL when he first came to see us. He had been following a very strict fat-free diet for years, which meant that he did not eat any red meat, eggs, or dairy foods, yet it seemed to have no impact on his cholesterol level.

We met with Raymond and explained our Restorative Medicine Program to him. Although he said he was very interested in trying it, Raymond refused to have his hormone levels checked, so we treated him "blind." He started on a Program in October 2004 with the following recommendations: 50 mg DHEA, 100 mg pregnenolone, and 100 mg coenzyme Q10 daily, all in the morning. In January 2005 he agreed to undergo a lipid panel, and his total cholesterol was 318 mg/dL and his triglycerides were 1,085 mg/dL. Encouraged by the improvement, Raymond agreed to the changes we suggested: increase DHEA to 100 mg/dL and pregnenolone to 200 mg. When he came in for his two-month follow-up, his total cholesterol had risen to 412 mg/dL, and Raymond admitted he had not been taking his supplements regularly. At that point we increased pregnenolone to 300 mg for one month and then to 400 mg one month later because he complained of severe short-term memory and joint problems.

In December 2005, Raymond donated blood during a local blood drive and when they revealed his cholesterol test results, we were all thrilled—it was 240 mg/dL, and this was not even a fasting cholesterol value. This was the lowest cholesterol level he had ever had. At that point, at the end of December, Raymond agreed to have his hormone levels checked, along with fasting lipid levels. The results were as follows:

Hormone	Reference Range	Raymond
DHEA-S	280-640 ug/dL	919 ug/dL
Pregnenolone	10-200 ng/dL	113 ng/dL
Estradiol:	0-53 pg/mL	55 pg/mL
Testosterone	241-827 ng/dL	274 ng/dL
Total Cholesterol	< 200 mg/dL	210 mg/dL
Triglycerides	< 150 mg/dL	518 mg/dL

Although Raymond still had room for improvement, the fact that his total cholesterol and triglyceride levels had declined so dramatically, and that we had been treating him "blind" with hormone restoration is testimony to the effectiveness of our Restorative Medicine Program. It shows us that even family history of high cholesterol is manageable by hormone restorative therapy. It appears that this condition develops as a compensatory reaction to low production of steroid hormones due to a congenital defect of the enzyme system that is responsible for the regulation of steroid hormone biosynthesis or their interconversions.

Hypocholesterolemia: Low Cholesterol

We don't hear much about hypocholesterolemia, which is the presence of abnormally low cholesterol levels. About 6 percent of the population in North America has cholesterol levels of 160 mg/dL or lower, which is the standard definition of hypocholesterolemia. This low level places individuals at greater risk for most cancers, hemorrhagic stroke, suicide, some gastrointestinal disorders, affective disorders (e.g., depression, schizophrenia), and coronary heart disease. Why is abnormally low cholesterol such a health risk? Because it is an indication of an imbalance of critical hormones.

Janet's story shows the impact that chronically low cholesterol levels can have on the body. This 29-year-old woman came to us complaining of severe fatigue, lack of energy, depression, anxiety, panic attacks, poor sex drive, obesity (5'6" and 242 lbs; 58% body fat), irregular menstrual cycle since her adolescent years, herpes on her lips, dermatitis around the mouth, and severe short-term memory problems.

When we asked Janet about her diet, she admitted that she ate a lot of "junk" food, including pizza, snack items, and ice cream. "I would like to lose weight," she said, "but I never have any energy. I'm just too tired to exercise. I really wish I could take diet pills that would take the weight off and not have to worry about a special diet." At the time, the only medication she was taking was Zoloft® for depression, and she said she noticed little benefit from it.

Janet's blood pressure was normal, but her blood tests revealed abnormal levels for other values, including a total cholesterol level of 130 mg/dL. All of her hormone levels were in the low end of "normal," and thus considerably out of range of optimal.

Hormone	Reference Range	Janet
DHEA-S	65-380 ug/dL	87 ug/dL
Pregnenolone	10-230 ng/dL	30 ng/dL
Total Estrogens:	61-437 pg/mL	87 pg/mL
Progesterone	0.2-28 ng/mL	0.4 ng/dL
Total Testosterone	14-76 ng/dL	33 mg/dL

When we recommend hormones for women, we always mimic their menstrual cycle. In Janet's case, her menstrual cycle was very irregular, ranging from menses every two weeks to once every three to four months. We focused on balancing her hormones related to her low cholesterol levels, and explained that we would not start her on a weight-loss plan until we had restored hormonal balance, which would take three to four months. Therefore we developed the following Program, with the recommendation that all supplements be taken in the morning unless otherwise noted:

- DHEA: 100 mg

- Pregnenolone: 100 mg

- Progesterone (50 mg/mL) gel: 0.25 ml daily during the first 10 days after completing menses, then 0.4 ml daily until menses and 0.15 ml daily during menses

- Vitamin E: 1,000 IU

- Vitamin C: 1,000 mg at bedtime

- Proprietary blend of melatonin (3 mg), kava root extract (250 mg), and Vitamin B6 (10 mg) at bedtime

We also recommended that she engage in aerobic exercise (e.g., brisk walking) twice daily for 15 minutes per session.

After just one week on her Program, Janet said she no longer felt depressed or anxious, and her panic attacks had disappeared, so she stopped taking Zoloft. At her one-month follow-up visit, we recommended that she use a one-month parasite-cleansing program because many of her symptoms were associated with parasites and she had several dogs in her home. Once she completed the cleansing program, we added several digestive enzymes to her Program for one month.

Two months after starting her Program, Janet came to her follow-up visit full of enthusiasm. "I'm getting my period every 28 days," she said. "That's the first time in more than ten years that it's been normal. And I'm sleeping much better, my sex drive is back, and the herpes has disappeared. I'm feeling so much better now that I can exercise—yes, I'm walking and jogging six days a week—and I've even lost 18 pounds."

At Janet's three-month follow-up, we reduced the DHEA dose to 50 mg per day, and we added the following supplements to help her with weight loss:

- Conjugated linoleic acid (CLA): 4 g before breakfast. CLA can reduce the deposit of fat and increase the breakdown of fat in fat cells.

- Chitosan: 2 capsules before lunch and two before dinner. This high-fiber supplement may help with weight loss.

- Hydroxycitric acid (HCA): 1,000 mg three times daily with meals. HCA may increase metabolism.

- Chromium picolinate: 200 mcg three times daily. Chromium picolinate stimulates the activity of insulin, which in turn helps with fat and glucose metabolism.

- Soy protein: one scoop daily before exercise

Because she was feeling so much better and was losing weight, Janet was motivated to change her eating habits. We recommended that she eat three to four small meals daily, eliminate all junk food, and eat her last meal of the day before 6 PM. During the first two weeks of her new dietary plan, we suggested that she substitute 400 ml of whole buttermilk for her last meal of the day.

When Janet reached her 15-month anniversary of starting her Program, she had slimmed down from 242 to 180 pounds. At this point she stopped using progesterone gel and we reduced her DHEA dose to 25 mg. That reduction, however, seemed to trigger a return of her depression, and in one month she regained 12 pounds. We suggested she increase her DHEA dose to 50 mg and also add 50 mg of zinc at bedtime and 1,000 mg of cat's claw daily (a powerful adaptogenic herb, which means it has a balancing effect and increases the body's resistance to the impact of stress). Her complaints disappeared over the next few weeks, and she also increased her exercise program to include running five miles daily.

Two and one-half years after starting the Program, Janet said her life had changed completely. "I'm holding steady at 146 pounds and my body fat is down to 18 percent. Since I had such terrible memory problems before, I was afraid to finish college, but this Program improved my memory so much I was able to finish my degree and finally get a job I really like. My family can't believe the changes I've gone through!"

Janet's improvement can also be seen in her hormonal profile:

Hormone	Reference Range	Before	After
DHEA-S	65-380 ug/dL	87 ug/dL	360 ug/dL
Pregnenolone	10-230 ng/dL	30 ng/dL	157 ng/dL
Total Estrogens:	61-437 pg/mL	87 pg/mL	454 pg/mL
Progesterone	0.2-28 ng/mL	0.4 ng/dL	1.8 ng/mL
Total Testosterone	14-76 ng/dL	33 mg/dL	61 ng/dL

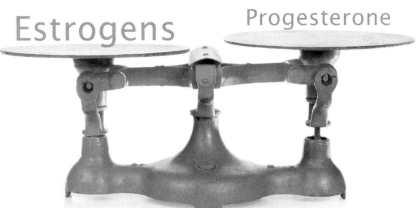

Estrogens   Progesterone

restore your balance...

Chapter 6

MENOPAUSE AND INFERTILITY

"I wasn't prepared for menopause," said Lorraine, a fifty-year-old interior designer. "I mean, I knew it was going to happen, but I thought I would just sail through it. But I was miserable: hot flashes several times a day, mood swings, and my sex life just fell apart. Sleeping became a problem, and I was always so tired that I often had trouble keeping up with my work. I even missed appointments with clients, and I found it increasingly hard to concentrate on my work. I certainly could not afford to have my job suffer, so I went to my doctor. He suggested hormone replacement therapy (HRT) because my symptoms were so bad, but I hesitated. I'm so glad I did, because then someone suggested I try hormone restoration therapy, which uses hormones just like my body makes, not artificial hormones or those that come from horses. That made sense to me, and so did the fact that all the hormones are restored to a balanced state. Within a few weeks of starting hormone restoration therapy, I felt much better because my hot flashes were nearly gone and I was starting to sleep better. After just two months I could barely tell I was going through menopause. This treatment approach was the answer to my prayers."

Menopause and andropause are natural stages of life in which the levels of the sex hormones decline dramatically in aging women and men, respectively. Menopause has garnered most of the media and medical attention for years, and it has only been in recent years that some physicians recognize the male equivalent, andropause. In this chapter we look at both of these natural conditions, the symptoms associated with them, and how the restorative hormone program can effectively address them.

MENOPAUSE

Some women look toward menopause with trepidation; they have heard, known other women, or read about the seemingly scores of symptoms that can accompany this change of life. Other women approach the transitional time with joy and anticipation of a life without a menstrual cycle or worry about pregnancy. Still others take a "wait and see" attitude.

The dramatic decline in estrogen and progesterone levels that characterizes menopause can have a significant impact on every part of the body, because these hormones can be found throughout the body, and they are themselves very potent. Because estrogens and progesterone have many competing effects, as we discussed in Chapter 3, it is especially important to keep these hormones in balance during this transitional period, to keep symptoms at bay and to make the passage into postmenopause as smooth as possible.

Signs and Symptoms of Menopause

As estrogen and progesterone levels decline and the desirable balance between them is lost, women can experience a wide variety of signs and symptoms. The impact of the imbalance on the brain can cause anxiety, depression, fatigue, mood swings, hot flashes, night sweats, insomnia, and a decline in sex drive. Dry skin is common, as are vaginal dryness and pain with intercourse. The impact on the heart can cause palpitations, increased cholesterol levels, and atherosclerosis. Weakness in the pelvic muscles can result in incontinence, and bone loss can lead to osteoporosis. The immune system can become compromised, causing a greater risk of developing some cancers.

(Mis)Treating Menopause

Although some women may argue this point, we believe menopause is a disease, albeit an *acquired* disease, as it has clinical signs and symptoms. That being said, pharmaceutical companies and many in the medical arena have convinced many women that they need to treat their disease with hormone replacement therapy (HRT), which typically includes non-bioidentical estrogen and progestins--which are hormone-like drugs, not hormones—to manage perimenopausal and menopausal symptoms.

For example, Premarin, which is often prescribed for women who have menopausal symptoms, is derived from the urine of pregnant horses, and consists of at least ten different estrogens, including one that is unique to horses called equilin.

Women are also prescribed other unnatural hormones as part of hormone replacement therapy, including other non-bioidentical estrogens and progestins that can be structurally related to progesterone (medroxyprogesterone acetate and nomegestrol) or testosterone (norethindrone and levonorgestrel). This approach to treating menopausal symptoms is usually done, by the way, without the doctors taking blood tests to determine women's hormone levels.

Natural Management of Menopause

A safe and effective way to approach this natural part of a woman's life is to use our Restorative Medicine Program and restore a proper balance to the hormones as she enters this new phase of living. We begin by taking blood samples to determine hormone and lipid levels, and then we develop a Program that addresses a woman's unique needs. Although our focus is on restoring balance to estriol, estradiol, estrone, and progesterone, we also note other hormone deficiencies and balance them as well, adding natural nutrients as necessary.

One very important factor to remember is that as men and women age, there are significant age-related changes in hormone production, and patterns of their release to the body. The goal of our Restorative Medicine Program is to provide a serum hormone profile that is similar to that found naturally in the body.

To illustrate how hormone restoration therapy can eliminate menopausal symptoms, let's look at Kay's story.

Kay's Story

When Kay came to see us, she was 58 years old and had entered menopause at age 53. She had retired at age 55 from her job as an administrative assistant when her symptoms became too much to handle. Her complaints included depression, lack of sex drive, severe hot flashes, sleep problems, muscle aches, hypertension, chronic fatigue, and being overweight by about 50 pounds.

Her postmenopausal symptoms were in addition to her primary complaint, however, which was migraine. Kay had suffered with migraines since she was twenty years old. In the beginning, the attacks had occurred once a month, but over the years they had gradually increased until she was having a migraine nearly every day of the month.

Like many migraineurs, Kay had tried to manage her migraines and other symptoms with over-the-counter medications, but she had not been successful. Around the time her menstrual cycle stopped at age 53, her doctor diagnosed Kay with high blood pressure and very high cholesterol (more than 300 mg/dL). He prescribed nadolol for the blood pressure and atorvastatin (a statin drug) for the cholesterol. Kay researched the side effects of both drugs, and after suffering with persistent stomach pains from the atorvastatin, and noting the risk of liver damage with use of the drug, she stopped taking it after two months.

When a friend referred Kay to us in 2004, she spoke to our advisors about our Restorative Medicine Program.

Impressed by what she heard, she immediately made plans to get her blood tested with her doctor. Her results were as follows:

Hormone	Reference Range	Kay
Total Cholesterol	< 200 mg/dL	300 mg/dL
Estradiol	19-528 pg/mL	19 pg/mL
Progesterone	0.2-28.0 ng/mL	0.4 ng/mL
Total Testosterone	14-75 ng/dL	51 ng/dL
DHEA-S	65-380 ug/dL	86 ug/dL
Pregnenolone	10-230 ng/dL	< 10 ng/dL

Based on Kay's medical history and her blood test results, we developed the following Program for her. All doses were taken in the morning unless noted otherwise:

- Pregnenolone: 200 mg

- Estrogens: Triest gel, formulated to 90% estriol, 7% estradiol, and 3% estrone, taken as follows: 1.0 mL on days 1 through 14 of each month, then 0.8 mL on days 15 through 25, then 0.6 mL for the remaining days of each month.

- Progesterone: micronized progesterone (50 mg/mL) gel used as follows: 0.8 mL in the morning and 0.4 mL in the evening for days 1 through 14 of each month, then 1.0 mL in the morning and 0.4 mL in the evening for days 15 through 25 of each month, then 0.6 mL in the morning and 0.2 mL in the evening for the remaining days of each month.

- DHEA: 50 mg

- 7-Keto DHEA: 100 mg

- Saw palmetto: 160 mg

- Zinc: 30 mg at bedtime

- Proprietary formula that contains 3.5 billion *Lactobacillus* group, 1.0 billion *Bifidobacterium* group, and 0.5 billion *Streptococcus thermophilus*, as well as gluten-free grasses, algae, natural fiber, herbs, and bioflavonoid extracts, one scoop daily

- Melatonin proprietary formula: 3 mg melatonin, 250 mg kava root extract, and 10 mg Vitamin B6; one capsule at bedtime

- Magnesium citrate: 420 mg at bedtime

Six weeks after Kay started her Program, she contacted us. Although we had requested that she call us after four weeks so we could make any necessary adjustments, she apologized about the delay, stating that she had felt "so great" and was doing so many things that she had let time slip away from her. Kay told us that she was free of migraine and hot flashes, that she had stopped taking her pain medications, and that her sex drive had returned. We suggested that she have her hormone and lipid levels checked again in about four months and to let us know how she was doing at that time. Ten months after starting the Program, Kay called to say that her total cholesterol was 195 mg/dL. She was completely free of her postmenopausal symptoms, was still migraine-free, and said she was exercising and losing weight.

INFERTILITY

Infertility is defined as the inability to get pregnant after engaging in frequent, unprotected sex for at least one year. Normally, after 12 months of unprotected intercourse approximately 85 percent of couples achieve pregnancy. Over the next three years, about 50 percent of the remaining couples will conceive spontaneously. Approximately 6 million people in the United States are affected by infertility each year.

Causes and Risk Factors

When attempts to get pregnant fail, the cause may be associated with either the woman or the man, or it may be the result of a combination of factors. Overall, the consensus is that the cause can be attributed to the woman about 40 percent of the time and to the man 40 percent of the time. In 20 percent of cases, the cause of infertility is unknown. Among women, the most common causes are the absence of ovulation (anovulation), blocked fallopian tubes, uterine abnormalities, or immunological causes. A history of pelvic inflammatory disease and endometriosis are also implicated. For men, the absence of sperm (azoospermia) or the presence of too few sperm (oligospermia) are the most common causes.

Some of the risk factors for infertility are similar for both men and women, others are not. They include:

- Age: A woman's fertility potential gradually declines after age 32, while in men it's age 35.

- Smoking: Smoking tobacco may reduce fertility and the possible benefit of fertility treatment. Women who smoke are more likely to have a miscarriage than women who don't smoke.

- Overweight: Women who are overweight and sedentary are more likely to be infertile than women who are not.

- Underweight: Women who follow a very restrictive diet and/or who have an eating disorder (e.g., anorexia, bulimia) are at risk for infertility.

- Excessive exercise: Some studies show that exercising more than seven hours a week may be associated with ovulation problems.

- Caffeine: Drinking too much caffeine may be associated with decreased fertility, although there are studies that find no correlation. High caffeine intake is more likely to affect women than men.

Conventional Treatment for Infertility

Infertility can be a very emotionally painful and frustrating experience for couples who have repeatedly failed at their attempt to get pregnant. Many turn to specialists for answers, and for some couples the answer is fertility drugs, including clomiphene citrate, leuprolide acetate, or human chorionic gonadotropin. Fertility drugs are the main treatment for women who are infertile because of ovulation disorders. These drugs are designed to work like natural hormones—follicle-stimulating hormone (FSH) and luteinizing hormone (LH)—to trigger ovulation. Intrauterine insemination is another option, while less than 5 percent of all infertility cases are treated with assisted reproductive technologies, of which in vitro fertilization is the most common.

Restorative Hormone Therapy for Infertility

We believe that the first step people should take when faced with infertility is restorative hormone therapy. Mainstream medicine has not yet caught onto the critical nature of this approach, yet there have been some inroads. For example:

- In July 2008, there was a report that DHEA had been used to restore ovulation in older women who wanted to become pregnant.

- In a 2007 study, researchers at Albert Einstein Medical Center showed that DHEA supplementation significantly improved pregnancy rates among women who were infertile because of diminished ovarian function.

- More than three decades ago, studies showed that there was a relationship between excessive androgens (e.g., testosterone) and the failure of women to ovulate.

- Low testosterone is a cause of infertility in men.

- There is evidence that stress can cause women to be infertile. Chronic stress is often associated with high levels of the hormone cortisol or an imbalance between cortisol and DHEA.

- Studies show that diminished concentration of total cholesterol and LDL fraction occur in women with threatened abortion. We believe that low cholesterol can be associated with low levels of sex hormones, and that may lead to infertility.

- The mind-body connection is also important in infertility. Men and women who have been labeled "infertile" often suffer from feelings of inadequacy, poor body image, and low self-esteem, which contribute to the stress level (and therefore changes in cortisol levels) and depressive symptoms.

Chapter 7

ERECTILE DYSFUNCTION
AND ANDROPAUSE

It's a condition that used to be a taboo subject. People whispered about it behind closed doors, and even then it was often a topic that caused much embarrassment. Today, however, erectile dysfunction (ED) is talked about freely on television and in other media. Formerly called impotence, erectile dysfunction is the consistent or recurrent inability of a man to maintain a firm erection long enough to have satisfactory sexual relations. It is a common disorder that affects about 50 percent of men aged 40 to 70 in the United States. At one time it was considered primarily a psychological problem or a natural part of growing older, but it is now accepted that ED is most often caused by physical problems. In particular, we find that restorative hormone therapy along with natural supplements can often resolve ED without the use of drugs.

Although ED certainly has an impact on a man's quality of life, the condition may also be the first warning sign of diabetes, heart disease, atherosclerosis, or other serious medical conditions. Therefore, we urge men who are experiencing ED to talk with their doctor about their symptoms and concerns.

What is Erectile Dysfunction?

Normal erectile function involves a complex set of interactions between the nervous system and the vascular system, and it all starts in the brain. The process of an erection begins when chemicals called neurotransmitters (e.g., epinephrine, nitric oxide) are aroused by physical or psychological stimulation. This causes nerves to send signals to the vascular (blood) system, resulting in a significant increase in blood flow to the penis. The two arteries in the penis provide blood to erectile tissue and to the corpora cavernosa, the two cylinder-shaped structures that run throughout the penis, which become engorged in the presence of the increased blood flow and pressure. Fibrous elastic sheathes cinch the erectile tissue to prevent blood from leaving the penis during an erection. When stimulation ends or ejaculation has occurred, pressure in the penis decreases, blood is released, and the penis becomes flaccid.

Causes of Erectile Dysfunction

Conventional medicine practitioners typically agree that erectile dysfunction can be the result of psychological and/or physical factors. In the psychological column, men who suffer from depression, anxiety, relationship problems, psychiatric diseases, or financial difficulties may attribute their ED to one or more of these situations. Generally, younger men who have ED can point to psychological causes more than older men.

Physical or organic causes may include use of medications and/or alcohol, cardiovascular disease, diabetes, high blood pressure, high cholesterol, penile injury, pelvic surgery, abdominal surgery, stroke, Parkinson's disease, spinal cord damage, multiple sclerosis, and prostate surgery, all of which can reduce or hinder blood flow to the penis.

What few physicians acknowledge, however, is the role that hormonal deficiencies or imbalances play in organic erectile dysfunction. Andropause is the time in men's lives when the decline in testosterone can have a significant impact on libido and on the ability to attain and maintain an erection. Erectile dysfunction is a manifestation not only of a deficiency of testosterone, but of imbalances in DHEA, pregnenolone, and progesterone, as well as nutritional elements such as magnesium and zinc. We talk about how to prevent and treat ED using hormone balancing and nutritional supplements below.

Before we do, however, it's important to mention other factors that can contribute to ED and which can be eliminated with lifestyle changes. These include stress management, not smoking, limited alcohol consumption, eating a nutritious diet, and judicious use of some medications, including certain antihypertensive, antidepressant, and antipsychotic drugs. Use of these drugs should be discussed with your physician.

Drugs That Can Cause Erectile Dysfunction
(Examples only; not an all-inclusive list)

- **Antidepressants, antianxiety, antiepileptics:** amitriptyline (Elavil), amoxipine (Asendin), clomipramine (Anafranil), desipramine (Norpramin), fluoxetine (Prozac), lorazepam (Ativan), nortriptyline (Pamelor), phenelzine (Nardil), phenytoin (Dilantin), sertraline (Zoloft)

- **Antihistamines:** dimehydrinate (Dramamine), diphenhydramine (Benadryl), hydroxyzine (Vistaril), meclizine (Antivert)

- **Antihypertensives and diuretics:** atenolol (Tenormin), bumetanide (Bumex), chlorthalidone (Hygroton), clonidine (Catapres), Furosemide (Lasix), guanfacine (Tenex), hydrochlorothiazide (Esidrix, Lotensin), labetalol (Normodyne), methyldopa (Aldomet), nifedipine (Adalat, Procardia), propranolol (Inderal), spironolactone (Aldactone), verapamil (Calan, Verelan)

- **Anti-Parkinson's drugs:** benztropine (Cogentin), biperiden (Akineton), levodopa (Sinemet), procyclidine (Kemadrin)

- **Cancer medications:** busulfan (Myleran), cyclophosphamide (Cytoxan), flutamide (Eulexin),

- **Histamine H2-receptor antagonists:** cimetidine (Tagamet), nizatidine (Axid), ranitidine (Zantac)

- **Lipid-lowering drugs:** statins: atorvastatin (Lipitor), fluvastatin (Lescol), lovastatin (Mevacor), simvastatin (Zocor); and fibrates: fenofibrate (Antara), gemfibrozil (Lopid), pravastatin (Pravachol)

- **Muscle relaxants:** cyclobenzaprine (Flexeril), orphenadrine (Norflex)

- **Nonsteroidal anti-inflammatory drugs:** indomethacin (Indocin), naproxen (Anaprox, Naprosyn)

Talk to your health-care professional about any medications you are taking, as this is not a complete list, and other medications, as well as combinations, may contribute to erectile dysfunction.

Hormones and Erectile Dysfunction: What's Going On?

You already know that hormone levels decline with age. Typically, aging is associated with reduced levels of total and bioavailable testosterone concentrations, a lower ratio of testosterone to estradiol, and decreased levels of DHEA, DHEA-S, thyroid hormones, growth hormone, and melatonin. In addition, a substance called sex hormone binding globulin (SHBG) increases with age, and this causes the concentration of free testosterone to decline and thus contribute to erectile dysfunction.

Mainstream Treatments for ED

Among the most popular treatment options for erectile dysfunction are drugs called phosphodiesterase type 5 inhibitors, which include sildenafil (Viagra), tadalafil (Cialis), and vardenafil (Levitra). All three work in a similar way: they block the enzyme phosphodiesterase and dilate the blood vessels in the genital area, which increases blood flow into the penis and helps to achieve and maintain an erection. These drugs have little to no effect on sexual desire. Sildenafil and vardenafil take effect in about 30 minutes and last 4 to 5 hours; tadalafil has an impact after about 15 minutes and can last up to 36 hours.

Like other pharmaceutical treatment approaches, there are side effects associated with use of these drugs. They include headache, blood pressure changes, irregular heart rhythm, flushing, vision changes, and nasal congestion, among others. The impact of long-term use is not known.

If ED is the result of psychological issues, behavioral therapy or sex therapy can be effective. Psychological therapy is often done in conjunction with medication and is more common in younger rather than in older men.

Men who do not respond to medication and/or psychological therapy are sometimes referred to invasive and/or mechanical means to achieve an erection, such as intracavernosal injections (e.g., prostaglandin and papaverine plus phentolamine), penile prostheses, vascular surgery, or vacuum/constrictive devices.

Hormone Restoration Therapy: Anthony's Story

It is our hope that more and more health-care providers will recognize the importance of hormone deficiencies or imbalances in the treatment and management of ED. Our experience shows us that an integrative approach to ED—hormone restoration and various nutrient and herbal supplements—can resolve this challenge. Our approach can best be explained by using Anthony as an example.

Anthony is a 54-year-old advertising account executive who came to see us in August 2000 with a 15-year history of severe impotence and lack of sexual desire. His other symptoms included depression, severe fatigue, muscle and joint pain, leg cramps, tingling and pain in his feet, sleep disturbances, and impaired short-term memory recall. He had had sex only four times in the last eight months, and each session had left him feeling severely depressed. At that first visit, his blood pressure was within normal range and his weight and height were average.

Before Anthony first started having problems with ED, he had been healthy and had never needed any medications. "I had always been fairly active, playing softball with the company league and jogging on the weekends," said Anthony, "My sex life was about average, I guess, so I couldn't explain the sudden change. I went to my primary care doctor, who then sent me to a urologist, but neither one of them could find any reason for my problem. So the urologist just kept trying different treatments, everything from methyltestosterone and testosterone pills, gels, injections, and patches to sildenafil and penile injections, but nothing worked. After fifteen years of nothing but failures, I was ready to give up."

Then Anthony's urologist suggested he contact us. Anthony was understandably skeptical, but as he said, "what did I have to lose?" At his first visit, we conducted a lipid profile and the results showed a very high cholesterol level of 330 mg/dL and a normal PSA. His hormone levels were as follows:

Hormone	Reference Range	Anthony
Cortisol (morning)	4.3-22.4 ug/dL	0.9 ug/dL
Estradiol	0-53 pg/mL	56 pg/mL
Progesterone	0.3-1.2 ng/mL	0.3 ng/mL
Total Testosterone	241-827 ng/dL	186 ng/dL
DHEA-S	280-640 ug/dL	92 ug/dL
Pregnenolone	10-200 ng/dL	24 ng/dL

You may wonder why, since Anthony had been taking testosterone for so long, his total testosterone levels were so low. One reason is that it is not enough to replace or restore **just one** hormone: you need to restore all complementary levels of hormones, and this had not been done for Anthony. Another is that some of the testosterone Anthony had been taking was being converted to less desirable hormones, such as dihydrotestoterone (DHT) and estradiol, which is demonstrated in the high estradiol levels in his test results.

Therefore, based on Anthony's test results, which showed very low values for testosterone, DHEA-S, progesterone, and cortisol, a relatively low value for pregnenolone, and a high number for estradiol, we developed the following initial treatment plan to restore his deficient steroid hormone levels and restore balance.

- Pregnenolone: 200 mg in the morning and 50 mg at noon

- DHEA: 200 mg in the morning and 50 mg at noon

- Testosterone: micronized gel (50 mg/mL), 1 mL in the morning

- Progesterone: micronized (50 mg/mL), 0.3 mL in the morning

- Androstenedione: 300 mg in the morning

We recommended a higher dose of DHEA than usual in Anthony's case because we wanted to not only restore the low level of DHEA but also to minimize the dose of testosterone needed. DHEA converts to testosterone, as well as androstenedione and androstenediol.

We also suggested the following supplements:

- Vitamin E: 1,000 IU in the morning

- Vitamin C (as sodium ascorbate): 2,000 mg in the evening

- Selenium: 200 mcg in the morning

- Saw palmetto: 320 mg with nettle root (240 mg) in the morning

- *Pygeum africanum:* 150 mg in the morning

- Zinc: 30 mg at bedtime

- Proprietary blend of oats, yohimbe, Siberian ginseng, and nettle, with mineral glandular extracts: 2 tablet twice daily in the morning and evening

- Proprietary blend of kava root extract (250 mg), Vitamin B6 (10 mg), and melatonin (3 mg): one capsule at bedtime

As we mentioned above, the increase in production of sex hormone binding globulin causes free testosterone levels to fall, so to prevent this we included nettle root in Anthony's Program. Nettle root inhibits the binding of testosterone to SHBG. Also, to prevent the conversion of testosterone to DHT, we recommended saw palmetto, and zinc, which block the 5-alpha reductase enzyme that is responsible for this conversion. Progesterone inhibits 5-alpha reductase, aromatase, and stimulates the activity of the parasympathetic system, which can lead to a release of nitric oxide from the terminal end of axons (nerve fiber that conducts impulses away from the body of the nerve cell). Nitric oxide diffuses into smooth muscle of the penile arteries. The arteries relax and blood flow increases into the organ. The spongy erectile tissue of the penis fills with blood, which leads to compression of the veins that normally remove blood from the penis, and all this results in an erection.

The addition of the blend of kava root extract, Vitamin B6, and melatonin was for Anthony's sleep problems, but the kava root also serves another purpose: it increases activity of the parasympathetic nervous system, which can result in a release of nitric oxide and vasodilation, in which the blood vessels widen from the interior, thus improving blood flow.

We asked Anthony to return for a follow-up visit in two weeks. "I was amazed," said Anthony. "After fifteen years of frustration, I finally experienced a dramatic improvement in my sexual performance. Just five days after starting the Program, not only did I have much more energy, but I was not impotent. My muscle pain was gone too."

The blood lipid profile we took one month after Anthony started treatment showed a total cholesterol of 243 mg/dL, a decline in estradiol to 31 pg/mL, and a rise in pregnenolone to 43 ng/dL, in DHEA-S to 340 ug/dL, in total testosterone to 396 ng/dL, and in cortisol to 16.2 ug/dL. Anthony reported that his sleep was back to normal and that he was much less depressed. There was also improvement in joint pain and in the tingling in his feet. Because of blood test results, and the fact that he was still having trouble with short-term memory, we increased his pregnenolone to 400 mg and his DHEA to 350 mg (250 mg in the morning and 100 mg at noon). At the same time, we added the following to his Program:

- Phosphatidylserine: 200 mg in the morning (for memory)

- Glucosamine sulfate: 2,250 mg in the morning (joint pain)

- Omega-3 fatty acids: 3,000 mg in the evening

- Chromium: 200 mcg in the morning

- B-complex: 1 tablet in the morning

At Anthony's six-month follow-up, his total cholesterol was 209 mg/dL and he said his symptoms continued to improve. We decreased the progesterone dose to 0.1 ml daily and added 7-Keto DHEA (50 mg in the morning). After one year of treatment, Anthony said he felt like a new person. His erectile dysfunction was a thing of the past, his other symptoms had resolved except for some minor joint pain, and his total cholesterol had dropped to 187 mg/dL. He continued his hormone restoration therapy and supplementation with glucosamine sulfate, Vitamins C and E but no longer needed to take the other supplements.

ANDROPAUSE

Andropause occurs in males and is characterized by low levels of androgens. The levels of testosterone, for example, can begin to drop in men as young as 35, and the decrease is gradual, typically 1 to 1.5 percent per year. This differs from the dramatic decline in estrogen levels that occur in women before menopause.

It is uncertain how many men actually experience andropause. However, according to urologist and sexual dysfunction specialist Michael A. Werner, MD, the incidence is estimated to range between 2 and 5 percent for men ages 40 to 49, between 6 and 40 percent for men 50 to 59, between 20 and 45 percent for men 60 to 69, and 34 to 70 percent for men 70 to 79. The reasons for the wide ranges are that different specialists use different minimum levels and means to measure androgens and to define andropause.

Some men experience the impact of the decline in testosterone more than others. Men who reach abnormally low levels of testosterone often report fatigue, depression, irritability, and reduced libido, symptoms that are similar to those experienced by menopausal women. Men who suffer from symptoms of andropause are typically treated by their doctors for a specific medical condition, such as depression, and then the underlying problem is not addressed. However, many men with andropause also have erection problems, including impotence (see "Erectile Dysfunction"), which is treatable using restorative hormone therapy and our Restorative Medicine Program. We approach treatment of andropause and erectile dysfunction in a similar way.

Chapter
8

MIGRAINE

"I suffered from migraines for more than 45 years," says Jean, from Springfield, Montana. "As time went on they increased in frequency until I had them almost every day. After tens of thousands of dollars spent on doctors and specialists, I still felt terrible. The migraines interfered with my life, work, family, friends, and vacations. Then I found out about your Migraine Program and my whole life changed. I have been on the Program for well over 3 years and I have had only two migraines since that time. Now I live a normal life. I enjoy foods that used to trigger my migraines, my blood pressure is normal, I have lost weight, many of my allergies have disappeared, and most of all I am enjoying family and friends without worrying about having a migraine. I can plan vacations and parties without having to wonder if I'll be able to go."

Some of the most gratifying results we've experienced with our Restorative Medicine Program have come from people who have migraine. Or should we say, **had** migraine. Jean's story is not unusual when it comes to the impact of restoration of hormones and nutrients and the rebalancing of various systems in migraineurs. We have treated scores of people who complained of migraine, and those who followed the Program have joined Jean's exclusive "club" of ex-migraineurs. To understand how hormone restoration and balancing can eliminate this often debilitating condition, let's start with an understanding of migraine.

What Is Migraine?

Some experts say that migraine is a primary disorder, which means that it is not caused by any other underlying medical condition. This one-cause, one-treatment concept would be welcome, especially to those who suffer with the condition. However, the truth about migraine, as we see it, is that none of the dozen or more theories about what causes it adequately explains the condition, or all the many laboratory findings and observations gathered about the disorder over the years. Before we look at our approach to migraine, let's look at some of the more popular theories proposed by conventional medical experts. A look at these theories can help you better understand how we developed our treatment program for migraine.

- **Constriction and dilation of blood vessels:** This theory is the most well-known. Dilation of the blood vessels was first suggested in the early 1850s by French scientists, while constriction was proposed about ten years later by a German physiologist. Both theories involve abnormal blood flow in the brain, and both are likely factors in migraine, but not all people with migraine experience these blood vessel abnormalities.

- **Role of steroid hormones:** Conventional research has shown that steroid hormones—which include those we use in our Restorative Medicine Program—play a major role in migraine. Studies show, for example, that migraine affects about three times as many women as men; that migraines occur during menstruation in 60 percent of women; and that use of oral contraceptives has an impact on migraine. Some of the major problems with the conventional approach, however, is that it does not recognize the importance of hormone balancing, nor the use of bio-identical hormones, nor mimicking the body's natural circadian (daily) rhythm.

- **Genetics:** The role of genetics comes in two forms. One, up to 90 percent of migraineurs have a family history of the disorder. Two, several genes have been identified as predisposing some people to migraine.

- **Serotonin:** Two things happen to the neurotransmitter serotonin during a migraine attack: levels of this brain chemical decline in the body, and high levels of it are released in urine. Serotonin has the ability to regulate pain signals in the brain and other areas of the body. It has been proposed that when serotonin levels decline during a headache, this triggers the trigeminal nerve (which runs throughout the face and head) to release chemicals called neuropeptides, which cause the blood vessels in the brain's outer covering to become inflamed, resulting in migraine pain.

- **Hyperexcitable brain:** An imbalance in the biochemistry of the brain can result in abnormal nerve cell activity. This is a condition known as hyperexcitable brain, which can be caused by various factors, including low levels of magnesium in the brain, increased levels of nitric oxide (which causes arteries to dilate), or mitochondrial abnormalities.

- **Impaired pineal gland function:** Serotonin and the hormone melatonin reside in this gland, which is located deep in the brain. Melatonin is made from serotonin, therefore low levels of serotonin results in low melatonin levels as well. People with migraine typically have low melatonin levels.

The True Cause of Migraine

Our research and experience has shown us that migraine is caused by a combination of neurohormonal and metabolic imbalances. That means the hormones we have talked about throughout this book (estrogens, progesterone, pregnenolone, testosterone, DHEA, cortisol), as well as dysfunction of the pineal gland and an imbalance in metabolism all work together to cause migraine and its symptoms. Migraineurs who follow our Restorative Medicine Program can eliminate their migraines. Here's how it works.

How our Restorative Medicine Program Can Eliminate Migraine

We have gained much experience working with migraineurs over the years and helped them eliminate their head pain and associated symptoms from their lives. During one of our studies, which ran for three years, we offered our Restorative Medicine Program to 21 women and 2 men who had tried unsuccessfully to prevent and/or treat migraine for a range of 2 to 36 years. Nearly 75 percent of them had tried hormone replacement therapy without success. All of the individuals complained of fatigue, 95.7 percent reported depression, 82.6 percent had insomnia, 73.9 percent suffered from gastrointestinal disorders, and 21.7 percent had fibromyalgia. These are all common complaints among migraineurs.

After we obtained blood test results from all of the study participants, we found that all of them had hormone deficiencies, with pregnenolone being the most prominent. The programs we developed were based on the unique needs of each patient. Overall, however, the program included the following elements:

- Hormone restoration therapy using hormones that are bioidentical to those produced by the human body, as we've discussed in previous Chapters.

- Rebalancing of the pineal gland using melatonin, kava root extract, and Vitamin B6. These supplements are often used for other conditions discussed throughout this book.

- Administration of magnesium citrate to restore the magnesium to calcium ratio.

- Balancing the digestive system with the use of probiotics, including organisms in the *Lactobacillus* and *Bifidobacterium* groups.

Now let's look at each of the four parts of our Restorative Medicine Program for migraine in more detail.

Restoring Hormone Balance

Women who are still menstruating make up the majority of migraineurs, and the menstruating years are especially characterized by fluctuations in hormone levels. Although all the hormones we have discussed thus far play a role in migraine, we want to focus particular attention on the hormones that complement each other. We know from experience, for example, that it is the balance between cortisol and DHEA, and between the estrogens and progesterone, and not the restoration of optimal levels of these hormones individually, that is necessary for elimination of migraine and the symptoms that accompany it.

Estrogen's relationship with migraine is deep and complex. We know that:

- The prevalence of migraine increase when a female's menstrual cycle first begins

- The decline in estrogen levels before menstruation triggers migraine in many women

- The prevalence and frequency of migraines usually decline during the second and third trimesters of pregnancy, when estrogen levels are very high

- Migraines usually occur immediately after a woman gives birth, as this is when estrogen levels fall dramatically.

It is necessary for the three main types of estrogen (estradiol, estrone, and estriol) to be in balance with each other, and the balanced estrogens collectively must then be in balance with progesterone for successful treatment of migraine to occur. To achieve that goal we recommend a formulation of bioidentical estrogens that is composed of 90 percent estriol, 7 percent estradiol, and 3 percent estrone. Although this is the most common formulation used, we make adjustments depending on the individual needs of patients.

Now let's look at progesterone's role in this critical ratio. Progesterone levels naturally fluctuate during a woman's monthly cycle. As women begin to miss ovulations with the approach of perimenopause in their mid-thirties and early forties, progesterone levels decline. This decline contributes to an imbalance with estrogen. This imbalance explains why the peak incidence of migraine for women is during the perimenopausal stage (between ages of 35 and 45). Therefore restoring a balance between these two critical hormones is necessary to prevent and/or eliminate migraine.

Rebalancing the Pineal Gland

Tiny but mighty: that's how some people refer to the pineal gland. Situated deep in the brain, this pea-sized gland plays a major role in the development and elimination of migraine. That's primarily because it produces melatonin, a hormone that orchestrates the body's circadian (daily) rhythm, including sleep patterns. (See Chapter 3 for a more detailed discussion of melatonin.) The association between melatonin, migraine, and sleep is well recognized: migraine is a response to an imbalance in the pineal circadian cycle, and problems with sleep can trigger migraine. Therefore, we have found that restoring balance to the pineal gland is a key factor in eliminating migraine, as well as the sleep problems, including insomnia, that typically accompany the head pain.

To restore balance to the pineal gland, it is necessary to supplement with melatonin, a hormone that plays several critical roles in the treatment of migraine. Melatonin:

- Helps synchronize sleep patterns

- Helps balance the activity of the endocrine glands (e.g., pituitary, testes, adrenals, ovaries, pineal) when they are under stress. When endocrine glands are under stress, production and secretion of hormones are affected.

- Has an effect on estrogen levels, which as you know has a key role in migraine

- Inhibits production of excess nitric oxide. People with migraine are hypersensitive to this element, which has been called "critical in the development of pain of migraine" by experts at the Brain Foundation in Australia. Indeed, many studies show that elevated levels of nitric oxide cause migraine and chronic tension headache. Nitric oxide is also a neurotransmitter, which means it passes along signals between neurons. Some of those signals are transmitted between neurons in the brain and those in the gut, where they can reduce muscles spasms in the gastrointestinal tract. Because of the important relationship between migraine and the gut, the presence of nitric oxide is key.

Most patients need to take melatonin for a few months only, which is typically enough time to restore the pineal circadian cycle. After stopping melatonin supplementation, some patients take it occasionally for a few days per month or every few months if they re-experience sleep disturbances.

Two other elements that help restore the pineal gland function are kava root extract and Vitamin B6. Kava root extract is derived from the root of *Piper methysticum,* and it is used by many people because of its ability to promote sleep, relax deep muscles, and provide a sense of tranquility. Similar to melatonin, patients who take kava root extract typically do so for only a few weeks, until they are migraine-free, and then discontinue the supplement, depending on how well their sleep difficulties have resolved.

Vitamin B6, also known as pyridoxine, is important because it aids in the production of serotonin, which, as we mentioned above, plays a major role in the sleep-wake cycle, mood, chronic pain, and appetite. Vitamin B6 also has a calming effect.

How to Balance Metabolism

Remember when we talked about the brain-gut connection in Chapter 3? The link between migraine (the brain) and the gut has been very well established, and that's why it is necessary to balance metabolism to successfully eliminate migraine.

The part of our Restorative Medicine Program that includes balancing metabolism involves using friendly bacteria, or probiotics, to maintain a healthy intestinal flora. Probiotics are bacteria that have health-promoting properties. The intestinal tract is home to both bad and good bacteria, and when the balance favors the bad organisms, that's when the intestinal tract becomes inflamed and causes symptoms such as diarrhea, constipation, abdominal pain, cramping, bloating, and gas. To treat these symptoms and prevent their recurrence, we recommend taking probiotics daily for several months to restore balance to the gut and to improve absorption. After that time, most people find they need to take probiotics only occasionally, perhaps once a month, to maintain a healthy gut.

The Magnesium/Calcium Balancing Act

Another segment of our Restorative Medicine Program to eliminate migraine involves restoring balance between ionized magnesium and ionized calcium. An ion is an atom or group of atoms that has a positive or negative charge because it has lost or gained one or more electrons. The term "ionized" here means that these minerals are freely circulating and always seeking something to which they can attach themselves and replace their missing electron(s). Therefore ionized magnesium and calcium are readily available to participate in various biochemical processes that can have a significant effect on the body.

Most people think of magnesium and calcium working together to keep bones strong, and they are right. However, the delicate balance between these two elements is closely connected to proper functioning of all cells, the digestive system, the activity of steroid hormones, functioning of the pineal gland, regulation of the sleep cycle, and prevention of fatigue.

Researchers have known for some time that low levels of ionized magnesium and a high ionized-calcium-to-ionized magnesium ratio are both associated with migraine. Therefore we recommend that patients with migraine take magnesium citrate, which is the type the body is best able to absorb.

To illustrate how our Restorative Medicine Program works for migraine, including recommended doses of the various supplements, let's look at Peggy's story.

Peggy's Story

Peggy is a 47-year-old woman who lives in Nova Scotia. When she came to see us, she explained that she had suffered with debilitating migraine for eight years and that sometimes she had to stay in bed for two to three days. Most of her migraines were accompanied by nausea and vomiting, and the pain had become so severe the last two to three years that she had quit her job as a paralegal. During her menses she would often have a migraine every day. Her menstrual cycle was regular at 28 days.

Over the years, Peggy had sought help from a variety of doctors, who prescribed medications that produced so many side effects that she stopped taking them. She also tried a detoxification method in which glutathione and Vitamin C are given intravenously, but it was not very successful.

In addition to migraine, Peggy had a history of chronic fatigue syndrome, severe depression, agitation, severe mood swings, sleep problems, premenstrual syndrome, anxiety with frequent panic attacks, and bloating. She had no sex drive and had not been sexually active for several years. Her internal medicine physician had diagnosed her with osteoporosis at age 45.

When she gave us her medical history, she revealed that she had been a vegetarian when she was younger, had been anorexic between the ages of 16 and 20, and had experienced episodes of emotional binge eating at other times. Currently she was 119 pounds at 5'6". In her twenties she had taken birth control pills for two years and had had two breast cysts removed. In past years she had noticed excessive body hair growth, but it had decreased significantly before the onset of migraine.

Peggy underwent a complete female hormone panel plus a lipid profile, and her results were as follows:

Hormone	Reference Range	Peggy
Total Cholesterol	< 200 mg/dL	215 mg/dL
Total Estrogen	61-437 pg/mL	409 pg/mL
Progesterone	0.2-28.0 ng/mL	22.6 ng/mL
Total Testosterone	14-75 ng/dL	45 ng/dL
DHEA-S	65-380 ug/dL	62 ug/dL
Pregnenolone	10-230 ng/dL	216 ng/dL

Peggy's case is a good example of how important it is to pay attention to details from a patient's personal and medical history along with the blood test results. On paper, Peggy's blood test results were good, except for slightly elevated total cholesterol and low DHEA-S. But Peggy had mentioned that she had experienced excessive body hair until the time her migraines started, at age 39. This indicated to us that at that time, she had had an imbalance of androgens—likely elevated testosterone. We believed that a higher than "normal" testosterone level was optimal for Peggy, so we raised all of her hormones, including testosterone, using the following initial Program. All doses were in the morning unless noted otherwise:

- Pregnenolone: 100 mg

- DHEA: 100 mg

- 7-Keto DHEA: 100 mg in the morning and 50 mg at noon

- Triestrogen gel (containing 90% estriol, 7% estradiol, and 3% estrone): 0.1 cc until the start of menses, then discontinue and begin again when menses stops

- Micronized progesterone gel (50 mg/mL): 0.4 cc in the morning and 0.4 cc at night for 10 days after completion of menses, then 0.6 cc in the morning and 0.4 cc at night until the first day of menses

- Micronized testosterone gel (50 mg/mL): 0.2 cc daily in the morning

- Proprietary formula of probiotics, green foods, and plant fibers: ½ scoop, gradually increasing to 1 scoop daily

- Magnesium citrate powder: ¼ scoop at bedtime, increasing gradually to one full scoop

- Proprietary formula containing melatonin (3 mg), kava kava (250 mg), and Vitamin B6 (10 mg), one capsule taken at bedtime

- Saw palmetto: 160 mg

- Zinc: 30 mg at bedtime

Peggy's case was somewhat different than many other migraine cases because the levels and ratios of hormones that were optimal for her were apparently greater than those needed by most people. Our plan to restore her hormones to higher levels paid off. After only one month of treatment, Peggy reported that she had not had a migraine, that her fatigue had improved greatly, and that she felt much calmer and less depressed.

Because she continued to have sleep problems and had developed occasional diarrhea and breast tenderness, we modified her Program by increasing her melatonin/kava/Vitamin B6 dose to two capsules at bedtime. Over the following months, we adjusted Peggy's Program occasionally, as needed. Five months after starting the Program, Peggy felt well enough to return to work part-time, and she also planned several trips.

Despite the fact that Peggy had experienced excessive body hair when her testosterone levels had apparently been elevated until age 39, she did not develop this problem again once we restored that hormone to what was optimal for her. That's because we restored and balanced all of her steroidal hormones.

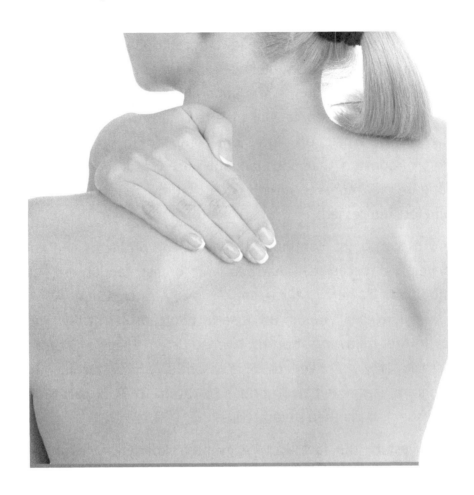

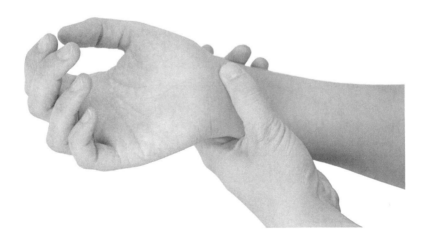

Chapter
9

ARTHRITIS, FIBROMYALGIA AND LUPUS

Various diseases classified as rheumatic conditions, including rheumatoid arthritis, osteoarthritis, Reiter's syndrome, fibromyalgia, gout, and lupus are all associated with a major decline in hormone levels and resulting hormone imbalance. This finding leads us to recommend our Restorative Medicine Program for individuals with these and similar medical conditions. In this chapter we explore our experiences with three of the rheumatic conditions that affect tens of millions of Americans—arthritis, fibromyalgia, and lupus.

Fibromyalgia

Fibromyalgia, once also known as "fibrositis" or "chronic muscle pain syndrome", is a chronic condition characterized by widespread pain, fatigue, and tender points. Approximately 6 million Americans suffer from fibromyalgia, and 80 to 90 percent of them are women. The disease usually develops during early or mid adulthood, although it does occur in children and older adults. People who have another rheumatic disease, such as rheumatoid arthritis or lupus, are more likely to develop fibromyalgia. Although the disease is not terminal, it often significantly diminishes quality of life.

A more detailed explanation of fibromyalgia is offered by the American College of Rheumatology, which established the following criteria for the disease:

- History of widespread pain, which includes all of the following: pain in the left and right side of the body, pain above and below the waist, and axial skeletal pain (cervical spine or anterior chest or thoracic spine or lower back). The pain must have been present for at least three months.

- Pain in 11 of 18 tender point sites when palpated with fingers with mild, firm pressure. Tender points are areas along the skin that are painful to the touch and which overlie areas of joint and soft tissue pain.

In addition, people with fibromyalgia typically have symptoms that can be classified as neuroimmunoendocrinological and include muscle and joint stiffness upon awakening or after sitting in a fixed position for a long time, facial pain (often temporomandibular joint dysfunction), headache, irritable bowel syndrome, memory lapses, confusion, burning or tingling in the extremities, allergies, restless leg syndrome, depression and/or anxiety, sleep disturbances, and hypersensitivity to sounds, light, or odors.

What Causes Fibromyalgia?

Scientists have been asking this question for several decades, and there are a few theories. Because fibromyalgia is a complex condition, the search for its causes has been complicated as well. One theory concerns the hypothalamic-pituitary-adrenal (HPA) axis, which we discussed in Chapter 3. It's been shown that patients with fibromyalgia may have a hyperactive or hypoactive HPA axis.

There is also a hypothesis that fibromyalgia is caused by an irreversible disturbance of the neuroimmunoendocrinological system. Without going into a long explanation, we partially support this hypothesis and believe that hormonal deficiencies in people with fibromyalgia are associated with a loss of sensitivity of cell membranes to hormonal impulses, which then leads to a dysfunction of the autonomic nervous system. The autonomic nervous system regulates function of the glands and muscles around blood vessels, and in the eye, stomach, intestines, bladder, and heart. The part of this hypothesis that we don't agree with is that fibromyalgia is irreversible. We have shown that it can be reversed.

Therefore, based on our clinical experience and analysis of the medical literature, we find evidence that fibromyalgia patients have a combination of neuroendocrinological and metabolic disorders and hormonal imbalances. For example:

- The fact that most people with fibromyalgia are women in their reproductive years suggests a link between the disorder and sex hormones. Fibromyalgia is also associated with delayed menstruation and reduced fertility, both signs of hormonal imbalance.

- Symptoms of fibromyalgia such as chronic and widespread musculoskeletal pain, gastrointestinal complaints, psychological problems, fatigue, sleep disturbances, and are similar to those experienced by people who have hormonal deficiencies.

- Fibromyalgia, migraine, irritable bowel syndrome, and related conditions share clinical, biochemical, and pathophysiological patterns.

- Women with fibromyalgia frequently have low melatonin levels, and supplementation with the hormone reduces pain, sleeping disorders, and depression in these women.

- Chronic stress, which is characterized by elevated cortisol levels, has been linked with the development of fibromyalgia. Abnormalities in neuroendocrine function may explain this connection.

- There are similarities between fibromyalgia symptoms and statin drug side effects, which lead us to believe these drugs may produce fibromyalgia-like symptoms by lowering cholesterol, which could lead to decreases or imbalances in hormone levels.

Conventional Treatment

Treatment of fibromyalgia focuses on alleviating symptoms, because there is no known cure for the disease. Doctors typically prescribe one or more of the following therapies to manage fibromyalgia: antidepressants, nonsteroidal anti-inflammatory drugs (NSAIDs), painkillers (analgesics), psychoactive drugs, lidocaine injections with or without hydrocortisone, physical therapy, gentle stretching, moderate exercise, stress reduction techniques (e.g., meditation, visualization), and cognitive-behavioral therapies. In recent years, there have been two drugs approved by the Food and Drug Administration for fibromyalgia: pregabalin (Lyrica®, December 2004) and milnacipran (Savella®, January 2009).

The Restorative Approach: Sarah's Story

Conventional health-care practitioners claim that fibromyalgia is irreversible, yet we have evidence to the contrary. We have used hormone restorative therapy to treat patients with fibromyalgia and their symptoms have disappeared. This supports our hypothesis that fibromyalgia is a result of hormonal deficiencies and imbalance, which results in a breakdown of neurohormonal and metabolic integrity.

Let's give you an example of a patient who no longer lives with the pain and disabilities associated with fibromyalgia. Sarah is a 55-year-old graphic artist who first came to see us in 2002 with a diagnosis of fibromyalgia from another physician. She had been diagnosed 15 years earlier and had not had a menstrual cycle for the last 13 years.

"It all started about 20 years ago," she says. "I developed pain in my back in the cervical and lumbar areas. I didn't think too much of it at first, but after a few months the mild pain in my back spread to pain and stiffness throughout my body. Then my problems just seemed to snowball."

Soon Sarah was experiencing severe fatigue, short-term memory problems, irritability and intestinal discomfort. Over the course of several months, migraine, insomnia, and severe depression were added to her symptoms. Visits to her doctor for diagnostic tests revealed no evidence of joint damage or disease, and she had no personal or family history of fibromyalgia or migraine to explain her symptoms. A rheumatologist diagnosed her condition as fibromyalgia, and she tried various forms of treatment, including massage, acupuncture, chiropractic, and exercise, with little or no improvement. She had also tried prescription medications for pain, depression, panic attacks, insomnia, and hot flashes.

"Nothing was working," she says. "I became so depressed I attempted suicide by taking an overdose of drugs in 2000. That's when my doctor put me on a few antidepressants, which really didn't help my depression or anxiety much, and did next to nothing for my other symptoms. I didn't know where to turn."

Then Sarah was referred to us by one of her coworkers, who had heard about our work with migraine. During her initial interview with us, she revealed her list of complaints: generalized pain, migraine, fatigue, poor energy level, severe depression, panic attacks, suicidal thoughts, insomnia, severe short-term memory difficulties, weight gain, constipation, and poor libido and sex drive. She was also taking a long list of drugs, including various painkillers as well as bupropion (antidepressant), clonazepam (antianxiety), zolpidem (for insomnia), and a combination estradiol/progestin pill.

We conducted a thorough medical and personal history and ordered comprehensive blood tests. The results of the initial blood tests revealed a clear imbalance: Sarah's total estrogen, progesterone, and pregnenolone levels were all low, and her testosterone was high in relation to estrogen and progesterone.

Hormone	Reference Range	Sarah
Total Estrogen	61-437 pg/mL	59 pg/mL
Progesterone	0.2-28.0 ng/mL	0.6 ng/mL
Total Testosterone	14-75 ng/dL	50 ng/dL
DHEA-S	65-380 ug/dL	100 ug/dL
Pregnenolone	10-230 ng/dL	32 ng/dL

Based on these initial findings, we developed the following treatment Program for Sarah. All doses were taken in the morning unless noted otherwise:

- Pregnenolone: 300 mg

- DHEA: 100 mg

- 7-keto DHEA: 70 mg taken at noon

- Triest gel (containing 90:7:3 ratio of estriol, estradiol, and estrone): 1 cc on days 1-14, 0.8 cc on days 15-25, and 0.4 cc on the remaining days of each month.

- Progesterone gel (50 mg/mL): 0.8 cc on days 1-14, 1 cc on days 15-25, and 0.6 cc on the remaining days of each month.

- Testosterone gel (50 mg/mL): 0.2 cc every other day

- Proprietary blend of melatonin (3 mg), kava root extract (250 mg), and Vitamin Bb (10 mg), 2 capsules at bedtime

- Proprietary powder blend of green foods, plant fiber, bioflavonoids, herbal extracts, and probiotics (3.5 billion *Lactobacillus* group, 1 billion *Bifidobacterium* group, and 0.5 billion *Streptococcus thermophilus* per dose), one dose (scoop) in the morning

- Proprietary blend of Vitamin C (1,860 mg as mineral ascorbates), magnesium (40 mg as mineral ascorbate), magnesium citrate (72 mg), calcium (100 mg as mineral ascorbate), Vitamin B6 (10 mg as Pyridoxine HCl), melatonin (100 mcg), lemon and orange bioflavonoids (200 mg) per two tablets; two tablets taken at bedtime

- Vitamin C: as sodium ascorbate, one 1,000-mg tablet taken 3 times daily

- Glucosamine sulfate: 2,250 mg

- Proprietary rheumatoid blend containing 10 mg undenatured type II collagen, devil's claw root extract, and bromelain: one capsule at bedtime with eight ounces of water

Sarah was able to discontinue taking her estrogen/progestin medication shortly after starting the Program. One month after beginning treatment she came in for a follow-up visit and was optimistic about her progress thus far:

"My migraine was definitely better, less severe and frequent," she says. "I noticed a real improvement in my back, neck, and joint pain, and felt a little less fatigued. I think that's because I was sleeping much better, and so I was ready to cut down on my sleeping meds."

Sarah also felt confident enough to discontinue her antidepressant and antianxiety medication at this point. Because she was still experiencing severe short-term memory problems and constipation, we recommended a few changes to her Program:

- 300 mg phosphatidylserine taken in the morning to support healthy memory. Phosphatidylserine is a substance found in all living cells, and it's most important function is as a building block for brain cells.

- 840 mg magnesium citrate (powder) at bedtime to promote healthy gastrointestinal (GI) functioning and eliminate constipation

- Increased her dose of the proprietary green foods/probiotics supplement from one to two doses daily to promote her GI health

- Use of a one-month parasite-cleansing program that contains herbs, fiber, and fructooligosaccharides, to support GI health

- Human growth hormone: 0.5 IU/day, six days per week

- Proprietary blend of herbs and homeopathic extracts to support sexual vitality.

After one month with the new additions to her Program, Sarah noted significant improvements. "The constipation and sleep problems were completely gone," she said. "I'm much less depressed, and I have so much more energy. And I can't believe that my sex drive is back—I feel like I'm in my twenties again, and my husband and I are thrilled. He tells everyone that I'm feeling 999% better!"

Four months after starting her Program, Sarah said that nearly all her original symptoms were gone or significantly improved. She no longer complained of fibromyalgia, migraine, depression, or fatigue. Her follow-up blood test results showed the progress:

Hormone	Reference Range	Before	After
Total Estrogen	61-437 pg/mL	59 pg/mL	249 ng/mL
Progesterone	0.2-28.0 ng/mL	0.6 ng/mL	5.4 ng/mL
Total Testosterone	14-75 ng/dL	50 ng/dL	62 ng/dL
DHEA-S	65-380 ug/dL	100 ug/dL	428 ug/dL
Pregnenolone	10-230 ng/dL	32 ng/dL	80 ng/dL

After more than two years on her Program, Sarah says she is completely free of fibromyalgia symptoms and other major health problems. She exercises four to five times a week and was able to return to work full-time as a graphic artist for her family business. She remains on hormone restorative therapy but has stopped taking nearly all the other supplements except Vitamin C; the probiotics when she experiences any GI problems, which is usually about once a month; and the proprietary melatonin/kava/Vitamin B6 formula if she has any problems with sleep.

Lupus

Lupus is a chronic inflammatory autoimmune disease, which means that the body's immune system attacks its own tissues and organs. Inflammation can affect many different body systems, including the joints, skin, heart, lungs, kidneys, and blood cells. The disease affects women far more frequently than men.

Lupus exists in four forms: systemic lupus erythematosus (SLE), discoid lupus erythematosus, drug-induced lupus erythematosus, and neonatal lupus. The most serious and common of the four is SLE, so we will focus on this form.

The signs and symptoms of lupus may develop suddenly or slowly, they may be mild or severe, and they may be temporary or permanent. A common characteristic of lupus are episodes called "flares," in which signs and symptoms worsen and then eventually improve or sometimes disappear completely for a period of time. Signs and symptoms of lupus generally include:

- Fatigue

- Fever

- Joint pain, swelling, and stiffness

- Butterfly-shaped rash (malar rash) that affects the cheeks and bridge of the nose

- Skin lesions that develop or worsen when exposed to sunlight

- Mouth sores

- Weight loss or gain

- Hair loss

- Raynaud's phenomenon—fingers and/or toes that turn blue or white when exposed to cold or during stressful times

- Shortness of breath

- Dry eyes

- Chest pain

- Easy bruising

- Anxiety and/or depression

- Memory loss

Causes of Lupus

The conventional view is that the jury is still out on what causes autoimmune diseases, including lupus. Some doctors speculate that people inherit a predisposition for lupus and then develop the disease when they encounter a trigger, which could be a virus, environmental toxin, medication, or other stimulus. In the meantime, some risk factors appear to include:

- Race: Lupus occurs more often in Asians and Blacks

- Exposure to sunlight: Ultraviolet radiation seems to trigger skin lesions in susceptible people, or possibly trigger an internal response.

- Epstein-Barr virus: This very common virus causes nonspecific signs and symptoms, such as sore throat and fever. Once the initial infection disappears, the virus remains dormant in the immune system unless it is triggered by some stimulus. Research indicates that recurrent bouts of Epstein-Barr infections seem to increase the risk of developing lupus.

- Chemical contamination: Some studies show that people who are exposed to mercury and silica, usually as part of their occupation, have an increased risk of lupus.

Conventional Treatment

Generally, doctors who use a conventional approach to treating lupus determine the severity of each of the signs and symptoms and then assess the benefits and risks associated with the different medications to alleviate them. Because lupus tends to flare, it is typically necessary to change medications and/or dosages as a patient's situation changes. Mild and moderate signs and symptoms are usually treated with:

- Nonsteroidal anti-inflammatory drugs, such as aspirin, ibuprofen, and naproxen sodium, can relieve inflammation, pain, and swelling. Side effects include stomach bleeding and an increased risk of heart problems.

- Antimalarial drugs, with hydroxychloroquine (Plaquenil) being the one most often prescribed. These drugs can relieve joint pain and swelling, rashes, fatigue, and chest pain. Side effects include muscle weakness and vision disturbances.

- Corticosteroids, which treat inflammation effectively, may also relieve fatigue and rash. These drugs can have serious side effects, including high blood pressure, increased risk of infection, osteoporosis, weight gain, and diabetes.

Lupus, Hormones, and Restorative Hormone Therapy

For several decades, physicians and scientists have known that sex hormones are an important component of lupus, but their exact role has remained uncertain. Clinicians often avoided prescribing hormone therapy for women who had lupus because they thought estrogens stimulated the disease. Recent research, for example, found that a short course of hormone therapy slightly increased the risk for more flares of lupus. This therapy used non-bioidentical hormones and did not address the critical issue of hormone balancing. A 2008 Johns Hopkins University School of Medicine study has noted that sex hormones, including DHEA, appear to play an important role in lupus, but again the role is not clearly identified.

Experience has shown us again and again that once we restore hormone levels using bioidentical hormones and selected natural supplements, the individuals who come to us with symptoms of lupus are free of their disease within a few months.

Arthritis

Arthritis is a general term for more than 100 different types of joint disorders that are characterized by inflammation. The literal meaning of "arthritis" is inflammation of one or more joints. Arthritis is classified as a rheumatic disease because its many forms tend to affect the joints, muscles, ligaments, cartilage, and tendons, as well as have the potential to impact other internal systems.

Of the many types of arthritis, the two most common are osteoarthritis (wear and tear of cartilage) and rheumatoid arthritis (inflammation resulting from a dysfunction in the immune system). Both of these forms, as well as other types of arthritis, have been shown to respond well to restorative hormone therapy.

Rheumatoid Arthritis

About 1.3 million Americans suffer with this form of arthritis. Rheumatoid arthritis is a chronic disease that is mainly characterized by inflammation of the lining (synovium) of the joints. The disease advances in three phases that typically progresses over a period of years. The first phase is the swelling of the synovial lining, which causes joint pain, swelling, redness, and stiffness. Then the cells divide rapidly, causing the synovium to thicken. During the third phase, the inflamed cells release enzymes that have the ability to destroy bone and cartilage, which damages the involved joints and causes more pain and loss of movement.

Because rheumatoid arthritis is a systemic disease, inflammation can affect parts of the body other than the joints as well. Some people experience inflammation of the lung (pleuritis), tissue surrounding the heart (pericarditis), the eyes and mouth (Sjogren's syndrome), or rarely, blood vessels (vasculitis).

According to conventional medicine, the cause of rheumatoid arthritis is unknown. Theories include genetics, environmental triggers (e.g., smoking, environmental toxins), viruses, bacteria, or fungi. The treatment approach according to conventional medicine typically involves a combination of medications, although other management techniques such as joint-strengthening exercises can be beneficial. Several classes of medications are usually used. One is first-line drugs such as corticosteroids and ibuprofen, which help reduce pain and inflammation. Second-line drugs, such as methotrexate, hydroxychloroquine (Plaquenil), and leflunomide (Arava), are also referred to as disease-modifying antirheumatic drugs (DMARDs). The DMARDs are designed to prevent the progression of joint damage, but they do not offer any anti-inflammatory benefits. Biologic medications (e.g., etanercept [Enbrel], infliximab [Remicade], anakinra [Kineret]) are more aggressive than DMARDs at stopping disease progression. These drugs work by intercepting a protein in the joints that causes inflammation. The biologics are expensive treatments and are associated with a significant risk of serious infection.

Osteoarthritis

Osteoarthritis is the most common form of arthritis. Although it can affect any joint in the body, it most often affects the hands, hips, spine, and knees. This form of arthritis is referred to as "wear-and-tear" arthritis, and it worsens gradually with time as the cartilage that cushiones the ends of the joints deteriorate. When the cartilage is completely worn, bone may rub against bone, which causes damage to the ends of the bones and painful joints.

What mainstream medicine proposes as possible causes of osteoarthritis—being overweight, joint injury or stress, heredity, aging—may certainly contribute to and aggravate symptoms of the disease. However, we believe osteoarthritis is related to the decline in hormone levels, because hormone loss is counterproductive to joint and bone health, and our experience shows that restoring hormone levels and balance eliminates or decreases symptoms of the disease.

Restorative Hormone Therapy for Arthritis

Our experience shows us that the decline in hormone levels is a major component in arthritis, and that restoring hormonal balance naturally is an effective way to manage this broad spectrum of diseases. As you have seen in the numerous stories throughout this book, it is common for individuals who come to us to have several major complaints, including joint pain, inflammation, and stiffness associated with arthritis. These symptoms disappear or significantly improve once patients take part in the restorative hormone therapy program.

Chapter 10

MACULAR DEGENERATION

If you have age-related macular degeneration, or if there is a history of this devastating and potentially blinding eye disease in your family, then the hypothesis and ongoing research suggesting that hormone restoration may slow and possibly even reverse progression of the disease will be welcome news.

Arlene thinks so. The sixty-nine-year-old retired accountant depended on her eyesight for more than 40 years as she first worked for a series of accounting firms, and then started her own CPA business. She retired reluctantly at sixty-eight when she noticed that she was having trouble with straight-on vision.

"I began to have difficulty seeing the numbers and reading, which I love to do, but my peripheral vision was fine," she said. "I thought it was just fatigue, but I made an appointment with my ophthalmologist anyway. He detected dry macular degeneration in my left eye and warned that I could very easily develop it in the right eye as well. He told me there was no cure and that hopefully the disease would progress very slowly, giving me years before I had to stop driving. He recommended some antioxidant and zinc supplements and sent me home.

Unfortunately, Arlene's case is all too common. An estimated 1.75 million Americans suffer from macular degeneration, often called age-related macular degeneration (AMD). AMD is the leading cause of vision loss and blindness in Americans aged 65 and older. Currently there is no cure for the disease.

We believe hormonal balance is a key factor in the prevention, management, and treatment of macular degeneration. Along with a good supplement program, we believe the challenge of this progressive disease can be met. First, let's take a closer look at the disease and how it affects the body and people's lives.

What Is Macular Degeneration?

Macular degeneration involves a deterioration of the macula, a part of the retina in the back of the eyeball responsible for central vision that is necessary to read, drive, watch television, and perform many other tasks safely and effectively. The retina contains millions of photoreceptors that capture light and sends them along the optic nerve to the brain, where they are converted into images. Macular degeneration occurs in two main forms, wet (neovascular, meaning new [neo] blood vessels grow in the macula area) and dry (non-neovascular), with the dry form accounting for 85 to 90 percent of patients with the disease. The less common wet type typically results in more serious vision loss.

Dry Form

The dry form of the disease is diagnosed when a substance called drusen accumulates around the macula and behind the eye, damaging the photoreceptors. Drusen is a yellowish material composed of cholesterol and decomposing tissue and metabolic waste. Dry AMD is also characterized by a thinning of the macular tissues. In about 10 percent of cases, dry macular degeneration leads to wet macular degeneration.

Although there is no Food and Drug Administration (FDA) approved treatment for dry macular degeneration, the National Eye Institute conducted a study in which experts found strong evidence that nutrients such as beta carotene, Vitamins C and E, and lutein may help prevent or slow progression of the dry form of the disease.

Wet Form

Wet macular degeneration is the more damaging form of the disease. The growth of new blood vessels beneath the retina is the hallmark sign of this form of AMD, and these vessels then leak blood and fluid that cause permanent damage to the retina. It is believed these new blood vessels form because the body is attempting to create a way to get more nutrients and oxygen to the retina. However, the attempt results in scarring, which causes vision loss.

Wet macular degeneration can occur in two forms: occult, in which the new blood vessel growth is not prominent and so leakage is less severe; and classic, in which blood vessel growth and scarring are clearly delineated, which results in more severe vision loss. Unlike the dry form of AMD, the wet form can be treated with several FDA-approved drugs, including fanibizumab (Lucentis), pegaptanib (Macugen), and verteporfin (Visudyne). The first two are administered via direct injection into the eye, while verteporfin is injected into a vein and then travels to the eye, where it is then "zapped" with a cold laser (called photodynamic therapy). All three approaches are capable of stopping vision loss, but they cannot correct any damage that has already been done.

Diagnosing AMD

Early signs of vision loss from AMD include abnormally fuzzy or distorted vision and shadowy spots in your central vision. Practitioners typically use an Amsler grid, which can identify the loss of central vision. Physicians also perform a retinal examination and may order a fluorescein angiogram to examine the retinal blood vessels that surround the macula.

Causes of AMD: Conventional Medicine Concepts

According to the National Eye Foundation and other sources, risk factors for AMD include:

- **Aging.** Fewer than 1 percent of people in their sixties have the disease, while this increases to more than 15 percent among people in their nineties, according to the *Canadian Medical Association Journal* (February 2004).

- **Smoking:** Numerous studies show that smoking is a risk factor for AMD. One of the most recent studies

(2008) followed nearly 5,000 people for 15 years and reported that smoking appears to be related to the long-term incidence and progression of the eye disease.

- **Poor nutrition:** Numerous studies show that a diet high in fruits and vegetables (and thus plenty of antioxidants) is associated with a lower incidence of macular degeneration. Thus a diet deficient in these nutrients—as well as omega-3 fatty acids—appears to be a risk factor for the disease.

- **Lack of exercise:** Research indicates that people who engage in vigorous activity at least three times a week reduce their risk of developing advanced AMD, compared with sedentary patients.

- **High blood pressure:** Several studies report that high blood pressure appears to be associated with development of this disease.

- **Being overweight:** Research shows that overweight patients with macular degeneration had more than twice the risk of developing advanced forms of the disease compared with people of normal weight.

- **Genetics:** Some researchers have identified an association between development of AMD and the presence of several variants of genes. One is called complement factor H (CFH), which Duke University researchers say may be linked to nearly half of all potentially blinding cases of macular degeneration.

Columbia University Medical Center investigators, along with others, reported in March 2006 that another gene variant, complement factor B, may be involved in the development of the eye disease as well.

The Restorative Medicine Approach

The hypothesis that hormones and AMD are linked is a revolutionary one for many people—including ophthalmologists--and it is exciting as well, because it opens up so many opportunities for effective prevention, treatment, and possibly even a cure for this disease.

Two of the strongest pieces of evidence that hormones play a major role in macular degeneration come together in the retina. One is the finding that DHEA levels are exceedingly low in people who have macular degeneration. As we have already discussed, when DHEA levels are low, other essential hormone levels often are deficient as well. The second piece of evidence is that the retina contains hormone receptors, and that the retina is capable of attempting to make its own hormones. We also know that the hormones pregnenolone, DHEA, testosterone, estrogens, and progesterone all have a role in the retina. Research shows, for example, that women who enter into menopause at a young age are more likely to develop macular degeneration, apparently because of the significant decline in estrogen levels. All of these findings point to a major role for hormones in vision in general and macular degeneration in particular.

Cholesterol and Drusen

Another link between hormones and macular degeneration concerns drusen. Investigative teams with several recent studies have identified cholesterol as a main ingredient in drusen. This is a pivotal discovery, because it links the hormone-maker cholesterol with the development of macular degeneration. The presence of cholesterol in the macula means the retina is attempting to produce hormones, and the presence of hormone receptors in the retina supports this theory. However, the retina and macula cannot manufacture the hormones (probably due to deficiency of enzymes), so the body continues to accumulate cholesterol in the area. The macula also attempts to get the hormones it needs from the blood, but there is an insufficient supply. The macula cannot convert the cholesterol into hormones and so the cholesterol gathers and forms into drusen, resulting in the eye disease. Another possible option here is the attempt of cholesterol to repair damaged areas in the macula because its function is as a reconstructive material. This process is very similar to atherosclerosis.

Although scientists are not certain why the retina and macula stop making hormones, it appears to be associated with aging and the natural decline in hormone production. Remember that the ability of the adrenal glands, ovaries, and testes to produce steroid hormones decreases with age, and this decline stimulates the liver to produce more cholesterol, which is an attempt by the body to create more hormones. Therefore, to avoid the production and accumulation of excess cholesterol, and in this case to avoid that situation in the macula to stop the formation of drusen, we need to restore hormonal balance.

Nutritional Support

Much evidence exists that specific nutrients such as the plant pigments lutein and zeaxanthin, Vitamins C and E, beta-carotene, and zinc have the ability to slow or stall progression of AMD. Three studies in particular yielded impressive results: the Age-Related Eye Disease Study (AREDS) conducted by the National Eye Institute; the Blue Mountains Eye Study; and the Lutein Antioxidant Supplementation Trial (LAST), performed by the Department of Veterans' Affairs, Medical Center Eye Clinic. Other studies point to the value of supplementing with omega-3 fatty acids to help stall this eye disease.

The AREDS study, which released its results in 2003, found that high doses of antioxidant vitamins and minerals (Vitamins C and E, beta-carotene, zinc, and copper) taken as oral supplements reduced the risk of progression to advanced AMD by 25 percent, and the risk of moderate vision loss by 19 percent. Since then, investigators have launched AREDS2, which began recruiting 4,000 participants in late 2006 for the five-year study. AREDS2 will build upon the results of the earlier study and also look at the impact of taking omega-3 fatty acids DHA and EPA (derived from fish oils), as well as lutein and zeaxanthin, two plant-derived pigments that accumulate in the macula and support central vision.

In the Blue Mountains Eye Study, which reported its results in 2008, investigators found that high intake of lutein and zeaxanthin reduced the risk of long-term incident macular degeneration. The LAST study also found that people with macular degeneration enjoyed improved vision when they took lutein alone or lutein with other nutrients (various vitamins, minerals, and antioxidants).

It is virtually impossible to eat enough foods to meet the high levels of nutrients you need to treat macular degeneration, which is why physicians often recommend supplements. Our Restorative Medicine Program includes specific nutritional supplements that complement the hormonal portion of treatment, which significantly increases absorption of nutrients, for macular degeneration.

Treating AMD with Restorative Medicine

Based on the evidence gathered thus far, which supports the relationship between hormones, eye health, macular degeneration, and cardiovascular health, we have developed a treatment program for this eye disease. The plan is designed to restore age-depleted hormones to optimal levels so that the macula can absorb the hormones it needs from the blood stream. It also incorporates nutritional supplements shown to reduce the risk of developing macular degeneration. In the meantime, we are conducting a research study to help clinicians and scientists better understand this disease.

ROZAKIS/DZUGAN AMD STUDY

In December 2008, we began accepting subjects for a study in which we will investigate the use of bioidentical hormones and their impact on the progression of macular degeneration. Candidates include people who have the dry form of macular degeneration or a family history of the disease. All recruited subjects must have 20/70 vision or better, using corrective lenses if needed. Participants will be prescribed hormones (estrogens, progesterone, testosterone, pregnenolone, DHEA, 7-keto DHEA), Vitamin D-3, zinc, and saw palmetto (for the prevention of testosterone convertion to DHT) in appropriate doses based on the results of their blood tests, which will identify the following levels: fasting lipids (including total cholesterol and triglycerides), pregnenolone, DHEA sulfate, total estrogens, progesterone, cortisol, total testosterone, Vitamin D, 25-Hydroxy, and PSA (for men, if value is not known).

Although various nutrients have been shown to be beneficial for people who have macular degeneration (see elsewhere in this chapter), in this study we will not be prescribing nutritional supplements because our investigation is to prove (or disprove) our hypothesis that hormonal restoration can arrest and/or improve this eye disease. If participants are already taking nutritional supplements, they can continue using them throughout the study.

Participants will be evaluated by an ophthalmologist every six months, and blood tests will be administered to monitor hormone levels six months after starting the study, and no later than 12 months.

Signs of success in the study may include (1) improvement in AMD, that is, slower progression or even reversal of age-related macular degeneration; (2) less conversion of the dry to the wet form of the disease; (3) better dark adaptation (faster adaptation from bright light vision to dim light vision); and/or (4) increase in best corrected visual acuity. The fact that hormones are much more powerful than vitamins gives us hope that the results will be significant. Preliminary results will be reported after one year of treatment, while longer-term results (i.e., conversion from dry to wet form) will be reported after three years.

Generally, the basic treatment program for people with macular degeneration is as follows:

- Estrogen: a gel (Triest®) compounded to contain 90% estriol, 7% estradiol, and 3% estrone. The recommended dose will vary depending on the patient's levels.

- Progesterone: micronized gel (50 mg/mL) at a dose customized for the individual patient

- Testosterone: micronized gel (50 mg/mL) at a dose customized for the individual patient

- Pregnenolone: as needed, dosed in the morning

- DHEA: as needed, dosed in the morning

- Vitamin D-3: as needed, dosed in the morning

- 7-keto DHEA: 25-100 mg, dosed in the morning and at noon

- saw palmetto: 160 mg in the morning

- zinc: 15-75 mg in the morning or before bedtime

- melatonin: 1-6 mg before bedtime

We have found that several nutritional supplements can greatly benefit people who have AMD. We have listed those supplements below along with the dosages we recommend, followed in parentheses by those recommended by the Age-Related Eye Disease Study, where applicable:

- Zeaxanthin and lutein: 3.75 mg of zeaxanthin and meso-zeaxanthin and 10 mg lutein per capsule, 1 to 2 capsules daily

- B complex

- Coenzyme Q10: 100 to 300 mg

- Krill oil: 2 soft gels daily

- Ginkgo biloba: 120 mg

- Grape seed extract: 200 to 300

- Bilberry extract: 150 mg

- Beta-carotene: 10,000 IU (25,000 IU)

- Vitamin C: 1,000 mg (500 mg)

- Vitamin E: 400 mg (400 mg)

- Copper: 2 mg (2 mg)

The Macular Degeneration/Heart Disease Link

A good example of the concept that many of the diseases we view as separate entities are in reality the same disease—the result of hormone and nutrient imbalance--can be seen with macular degeneration and cardiovascular disease. An Australian study published in 2008 reported that people who had macular degeneration had a five-fold higher risk of dying of cardiovascular disease and a ten-fold greater risk of dying of stroke. After the investigators took into account the traditional cardiovascular risk factors, having AMD predicted a twofold risk of death from cardiovascular disease.

Beyond Macular Degeneration

Although we have focused on the use of restorative hormones for macular degeneration in this chapter, we also want to mention that based on our experience over the last four years, we believe everyone older than 40 should pursue restorative hormone therapy whether they have macular degeneration or not. People who are presbyopic (need bifocals) are about age 44 and are also hormone deficient. This is an ideal time to teach the great benefits from restoration and balancing of hormones. Balancing hormones would also conceivably help with other vision problems that typically occur with age, including glaucoma and cataracts.

Chapter 11

PSYCHOLOGICAL DISORDERS

Psychological (mental) disorders are common in the United States: more than 26 percent of Americans ages 18 and older suffer from a diagnosable mental disorder in a given year. This translates into approximately 60 million people who are living with a psychological condition. Many people suffer from more than one mental disorder at a time; in fact, about 45 percent of people who have a mental disorder meet the criteria for two or more conditions.

In addition, some psychological disorders are commonly associated with other medical conditions. Depression and anxiety are two psychological diagnoses that often accompany other medical conditions. For example, people with migraine often also have depression and/or anxiety, as do people who have fibromyalgia, heart disease, erectile dysfunction, gastrointestinal disorders, cancer, menopause, or andropause.

Our experience in treating psychological disorders, especially depression and anxiety, has been that these conditions disappear or significantly improve in people whom we treat that come to us complaining primarily of another health concern, such as those we just named. Is this coincidence? We think not.

In fact, many experts in conventional medicine are conducting research and gathering evidence that supports the role of certain hormones in the cause and treatment of depression and other psychological disorders. Some of that research is explained below. What has yet to occur, however, is for them to acknowledge that these mental conditions can be treated successfully by achieving hormonal balance using hormones that are bioidentical to those produced by the human body.

In this chapter we explore the role of hormone restoration in several important psychological conditions that affect millions of Americans: attention deficit/hyperactivity disorder, antisocial behavior, autism, and depression.

Attention-Deficit Hyperactivity Disorder

One of the most distressing and common types of behavioral disorders that affect children and adolescents is attention-deficit/ hyperactivity disorder (ADHD). The disorder affects approximately 3 to 10 percent of boys and girls aged 18 and younger, with boys affected more than girls. Although the prevalence of ADHD does decline as people enter adulthood, about 65 percent of children with ADHD still experience symptoms as adults. Thus an estimated 2 to 7 percent of adults in the United States have ADHD.

What is ADHD?

ADHD is a complex psychiatric disorder that is characterized by limited attention, impulsivity, and overactivity. The condition can be broken down into three types, which identifies the main characteristic of the affected individual: predominantly inattentive, predominantly hyperactive-impulsive, and a combination of the two. Both impulsivity and inattention tend to grow more prominent with age, while hyperactivity usually declines in adolescence.

Conventional medical research has not identified the precise causes of ADHD. Several theories have been proposed, including environmental factors (e.g., exposure to lead, cigarette smoke, or alcohol during pregnancy) and genetics (about 40 to 50 percent of children with ADHD have a parent or other close relative with the condition).

Many people who have ADHD also have other psychiatric conditions, which can complicate both diagnosis and treatment. Comorbidity (having two or more diagnoses at the same time) between ADHD and social anxiety disorder occurs in about 25 percent of cases. Social anxiety disorder is the third most common mental health disorder, affecting about 10 million Americans. This condition is characterized by an intense fear of social situations, depression, and lack of self-esteem.

Conventional Approach to Treatment

The conventional treatment approach to ADHD usually includes parental education, behavioral therapy, placement of children in the most appropriate educational environment, and prescription medications. On the latter, the most commonly used drugs include psychostimulants, antidepressants, and alpha-adrenergic agonists. Among the most commonly used psychostimulants are methylphenidate (Ritalin®, Concerta®, dextroamphetamine/ amphetamine (Adderall®) and dextroamphetamine (Dexedrine®). These drugs are associated with side effects that include weight loss, sleep disturbances, decreased appetite, and irritability. Some heart-related deaths have also been reported.

A nonstimulant medication called atomoxetine (Strattera®) is used for ADHD symptoms as well as anxiety. Side effects can include nausea, sedation, weight loss, and reduced appetite. In rare cases, use of atomoxetine has also been linked to liver problems and even suicidal tendencies.

Treatment of social anxiety disorder focuses on use of prescription medications (e.g., antidepressants, beta-blockers) and psychotherapy. These approaches, like those for ADHD, are typically of limited effectiveness.

ADHD and Hormone Restoration Therapy

Our work with ADHD and social anxiety disorder has shown us that these psychiatric/behavioral disorders can be treated successfully without the use of pharmaceuticals. Unfortunately, most parents have been convinced by the medical community that prescription drugs are the most effective way to treat their children. We believe that our success with hormone restoration and nutritional supplementation, however, offers hope to millions of young people and adults who have been trapped into thinking they must depend on prescription medications to "get through the day."

To demonstrate the effectiveness of hormone and nutritional therapy, we tell you about Bradley, a young man who had been diagnosed with both ADHD and social anxiety disorder.

Bradley's Story

Bradley first came to see us in December 2002 when he was 24 years old. He had been diagnosed with ADHD at age seven and with social anxiety disorder at age 14. At 5'8" he weighed in at 178 pounds and had a slightly higher than normal percentage of body fat (23%; normal is 14 to 20%). His blood pressure was 110/75 mmHg and his pulse, 60 beats per minute.

Bradley's main complaints when he first saw us were severe fatigue and low energy level, decreased appetite, major depression, severe anxiety, poor short-term memory, sleep problems, poor libido, sore throat, and frequent sinus infections. He explained that being in social situations made his "heart race" and that he broke out in a sweat. He confessed that he was not physically active because of his low energy level.

During his first visit with us, Bradley told us that his current medications included the antidepressant paroxetine

(Paxil®) and a psychostimulant, methylphenidate (Ritalin®). In previous years he had been prescribed several other antidepressants that he no longer took. After we gathered all his medical information, he had blood tests taken to determine his hormone and lipid levels.

The test results were as follows:

Hormone	Reference Range	Anthony
Total Cholesterol	< 200 mg/dL	195 mg/dL
Total Testosterone	241-827 ng/dL	678 ng/dL
DHEA-S	280-640 ug/dL	79 ug/dL
Pregnenolone	10-200 ng/dL	56 ng/dL

Bradley's DHEA-S levels were extremely low, and the pregnenolone level was poor. Based on these results, we recommended the following initial treatment program. All doses were taken in the morning unless noted otherwise:

- Pregnenolone: 100 mg

- DHEA: 100 mg

- 7-keto DHEA: 70 mg

- Androstenedione: 50 mg, 30 minutes before exercise for two months

- Vitamin E: 800 IU

- Proprietary blend: melatonin (3 mg), kava root extract (250 mg), and Vitamin B6 (10 mg), one capsule at bedtime for sleep

- Zinc: 60 mg at bedtime

- Proprietary blend: Vitamin C (1,860 mg as mineral ascorbates), magnesium (40 mg as mineral ascorbate), magnesium citrate (72 mg), calcium (100 mg as mineral ascorbate), Vitamin B6 (10 mg as Pyridoxine HCl), melatonin (100 mcg), lemon and orange bioflavonoids (200 mg) per two tablets; two tablets at bedtime

- Tribulus terrestris: two 450-mg tablets chewed (for libido)

Bradley reported back to us in two months and said he could not believe the difference. His energy level had improved significantly, so much so that he was able to exercise four to five days a week. He had stopped taking his antidepressant during the first two weeks of starting our program and said that he no longer felt anxious, depressed, or restless. He said his sex drive was good and so was his performance.

At this point we suggested that he stop taking the androstenedione, both of the proprietary blends taken at bedtime, and the Tribulus terrestris. We also recommended that he decrease his DHEA to 50 mg, the zinc to 30 mg, and the Vitamin E to 400 IU. The only item we added to the Program was 210 mg of magnesium citrate at bedtime.

One year later, Bradley contacted us and said he was still feeling great. He was continuing with his exercise program, he had had no recurrence of any of his ADHD or social anxiety disorder symptoms, nor any of his other problems. He was still taking 50 mg of pregnenolone and 25 mg of DHEA intermittently, but otherwise felt no need for other supplements.

Joshua's Story

Joshua is a six-year-old boy who was diagnosed with severe ADHD at age 4, and he was a major behavioral challenge for his parents. We tested Joshua and found that he had extremely low hormone levels. His test results are given here:

Hormone	Reference Range	Joshua
Total Cholesterol	100-189 mg/dL	108 mg/dL
Total Testosterone	0-20 ng/dL	16 ng/dL
DHEA-S	< 186 ug/dL	< 15 ug/dL
Pregnenolone	10-200 ng/dL	41 ng/dL
Estradiol	0-53 pg/mL	< 10 pg/mL
Progesterone	0.3-1.2 ng/mL	0.4 ng/mL

Joshua's severe deficiency of DHEA places him in a significant imbalance with the stress hormone, cortisol. As we have discussed previously, a balanced DHEA:cortisol ratio is critical to maintain physical and emotional health. His extremely low estradiol levels also put Joshua significantly out of balance with testosterone. Given these hormone level results, it is no surprise that Joshua has a severe case of ADHD.

In Joshua's case, we would recommend initially giving pregnenolone and DHEA to help stabilize his psychological status. The pregnenolone can also convert to progesterone, which has a calming effect. The DHEA would help to both restore the balance with cortisol and for its possible conversion to estradiol. The estradiol is critical because it needs to reach an optimal balance with testosterone to help manage aggression and hyperactivity.

We did not treat Joshua because his parents, who were working with a team of conventional pediatricians, were swayed by the assurances by their doctors that prescription medications were the best route. However, we believe that this child clearly needs an orchestrated program of hormones and nutritional supplements.

What Pediatricians Need to Learn

One important lesson to take away from Joshua's case is that hormone deficiencies can occur at any age. Another is, given this fact, pediatricians should consider testing for hormone deficiencies when they are faced with children who are displaying the signs and symptoms of psychiatric problems such as ADHD, social anxiety disorder, bipolar disorder, obsessive-compulsive disorder, and other behavioral problems. If these children were diagnosed with type 1 diabetes (a deficiency of the hormone insulin), they would be prescribed insulin immediately. If they showed a deficiency of thyroid hormone, a prescription for thyroid hormone would be written posthaste.

But when pediatricians are presented with children with behavioral challenges, they prescribe drugs, drugs that not only do nothing to address the root cause of the psychological problems—hormone imbalance--but also introduce harmful side effects. Doctors who deal with such children must remember this simple truth: our bodies do not produce drugs, and have no deficiencies related to them. Yet it is widely known among medical professionals that neurosteroids (e.g., pregnenolone, DHEA, progesterone) are extremely important for normal brain function because they impact various neurophysiological and behavioral processes. It is also common knowledge that cholesterol is the precursor for these and other essential steroidal hormones. Therefore, pediatricians who elect to recognize the power of hormone restoration in behavioral problems could completely turn around how behavioral disorders are diagnosed and treated.

The Role of Hormone Restoration in ADHD

We are not saying that hormone restoration can definitively cure ADHD and other psychological disorders. However, we firmly believe that this treatment approach can significantly improve the lives of people who suffer with these conditions and free them from a possible lifetime of taking prescription medications that can play havoc with their body chemistry. The long-term impact of taking drugs for ADHD into adulthood has not been determined. Some studies show that the drugs can hinder the growth of children who take them. Our Restorative Medicine Program, however, helps bring the body back to its natural state of balance and health.

Depression

You may recall the Women's Health Initiative (WHI; see Chapter 3), in which middle-aged women took estrogen (non-bioidentical) replacement therapy. The study was discontinued when it was determined that this treatment program was causing a significant increased risk of breast cancer, stroke, blood clots, and dementia in the treated women.

Another finding emerged from the study, but it was not one researchers had been looking for. Within two months of publication of the WHI results, experts noted that women who had had a long history of depression before entering the study, and who had gone into remission during the study, were now experiencing a reemergence of their depressive symptoms. It was apparent that estrogen supplementation—albeit non-bioidentical estrogen in this case—had a positive impact on depressive symptoms. This incidence is not the only proof.

Numerous studies have shown that estrogen replacement therapy generally relieves mood swings in perimenopausal women who have vasomotor instability (unstable constriction and dilation of the blood vessels, which can result in hot flashes, cold hands and feet, etc). Several studies have shown that natural estrogens such as 17beta-estradiol offer antidepressive relief for women who have major depressive disorder and those who suffer with depression during perimenopause. In fact, estradiol treatment resulted in complete remission in most of the patients studied.

DHEA, Cortisol, and Depression

In a British study published in 2009, for example, the researchers indicate the importance of the cortisol/DHEA ratio in treatment-resistant depression. As we explained in Chapter 2, there is a critically significant relationship between cortisol and DHEA, and it is important to maintain a balance between these two hormones for health. Just how important this balance is has been demonstrated in recent studies of antisocial behavior.

Antisocial Behavior

What if antisocial behavior could be treated with hormones? What if we could help resolve the rise of violent crime with restorative hormone therapy? Sound farfetched? Perhaps not.

A recent Cambridge University study found that low levels of the stress hormone cortisol were associated with antisocial behavior in adolescent boys. While cortisol levels usually rise during stressful situations, which helps people regulate their emotional responses—especially violent behaviors--the study found that boys with a history of severe antisocial behavior did not experience this increase in the hormone level. That means when these adolescents are in a highly stressful situation, the body does not respond appropriately and give them the hormones they need to cope with their environment. Thus, some bad behaviors may be a form of mental illness that is based on a chemical (hormone) imbalance in the brain.

In the study, two groups of adolescent boys were placed in a stressful experimental situation designed to cause frustration. The investigators took samples of saliva before, during, and after the experiment to measure cortisol levels during each phase. While normal adolescents had large increases in cortisol levels when they were frustrated, those who had a history of severe antisocial behavior had a significant drop in cortisol levels. This is a critical finding, because the rise in cortisol during stressful situations helps people regulate and control their emotions, including temper and violent behaviors. Because the boys with antisocial behaviors experienced a decline rather than a rise in cortisol, they do not have the chemical "tools" to cope with stress. The study results strongly suggest that antisocial behavior is more biologically based than previously thought, and that hormone restoration may be an effective preventive and/or treatment for such cases.

Developmental Disorders: Autism

Developmental disorders are a diverse group of severe, chronic conditions that involve mental and/or physical disabilities. People who have a developmental disability have difficulties with activities such as learning, language, socialization, mobility, self-help, and independent living. The more common types of developmental disabilities include autism spectrum disorders, cerebral palsy, hearing loss, and mental retardation. We will focus on the most common of the autism spectrum disorders, autism.

Autism

Experts estimate that autism affects approximately three to six children out of every 1,000 in the United States. This developmental disorder is characterized by significant problems with social interaction, verbal and nonverbal communication, and concentration, as well as unusual, repetitive, or severely limited behaviors and interests. One of the most prevalent group of developmental disabilities is autism spectrum disorders, which include disabilities that involve significant problems in communication and social interactions, as well as unusual behaviors and interests. Many individuals who have an autism spectrum disorder also have difficulty with learning, concentration, and in reacting appropriately to different sensations and situations. Autism spectrum disorders typically develop before the age of three years and persist throughout a lifetime. Males are affected approximately four times more than females.

The ability of the Restorative Hormone Program to have a positive impact on autism came to our attention when the parents of a fourteen-year-old girl came to us, asking if we could help their daughter. Here is her story.

Clara's Story

Clara is a fourteen-year-old girl who had been diagnosed with a seizure disorder at age four months. The disorder involves generalized and multiple seizures, and at the time she came to see us she was taking Sabril, Topamax, clonazepam, and clorazepate for the seizures. She also had been diagnosed with autism, is unable to speak, and is developmentally delayed. Other signs and symptoms included severe constipation, mood swings, great difficulty concentrating, and poor overall physical condition. She was believed to be experiencing migraines, but because she cannot speak, her parents and other physicians had come to this conclusion because she hits her head repeatedly and cries. The headaches occur almost daily in the morning and sometimes in the afternoon as well. Her parents noted that about four to six days a month she does not appear to have the headaches. Although she had not yet started menstruating when we first saw her, we suspected she could have premenstrual-like syndrome because of her tendency to cry more often on some days than others.

When she was an infant, she underwent CAT (computed tomography) scans which did not show any abnormalities until 2006, when a scan showed a Chiari malformation, a condition in which brain tissue protrudes into the spinal canal, and she underwent surgery in October of that year to remedy the problem.

Clara's case was an unusually complex one, and we consulted with the patient's neurologist and family extensively before she entered the Program so that everyone had reasonable expectations about the outcome of therapy. With that in mind, Clara had her initial laboratory tests done, and the results were as follows:

Hormone	Reference Range	Clara
Total Cholesterol	100-169 mg/dL	153 mg/dL
Total Testosterone	14-76 ng/dL	44 ng/dL
DHEA-S	65-380 ug/dL	193 ug/dL
Pregnenolone	10-230 ng/dL	82 ng/dL
Progesterone	0.2-28 ng/mL	0.9 ng/mL
Total Estrogen	Pre-pubertal: < 40 pg/mL	69 pg/mL
Homocysteine	0-15 umol/L	4.3 umol/L

Once we had Clara's lab results, we recommended the following initial Program for her:

- DHEA 7-Keto: 25 mg at noon
- Pregnenolone: 25 mg in morning, 15 mg at noon
- B complex: use half capsule
- Magna-Calm, ¼ scoop in the morning and 2/3 scoop in the evening.
- SAMe: 200 mg capsules twice daily

- MetaRest: one capsule daily for 2 weeks, then open capsule and use half of powder 30 minutes before bedtime

- ProGreens, 1/3 scoop in favorite drink in the morning

- Zinc, 15 mg in the evening

The family waited six months before reporting back to us about any progress. The reason, they said, was that "we are always so guarded in reporting good news as historically it doesn't last. I am so happy to have our little girl happy. She is having so many happy, smiling interactive days." Thus their report at six months was that Clara's head hitting had decreased as early as two weeks after she started treatment, and since then they had been able to reduce the amount of Vicodin their daughter needed. In fact, some weeks she did not need the medication at all. The family also was thrilled that Clara was watching television instead of banging on it, and friends and family had noticed a big difference in Clara's behavior as well.

Clara's case is a complex one, but her family is optimistic about further improvements. They are very open to our suggestions and recommendations on how to reduce Clara's seizures and other complications, and we continue to work with them.

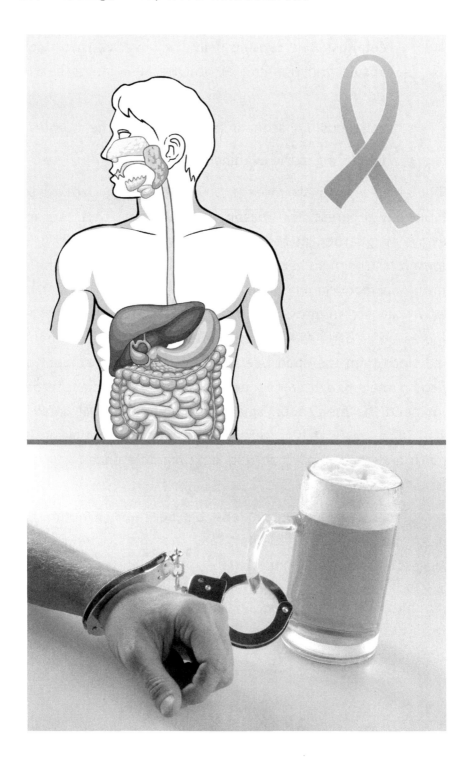

Chapter
12

OTHER DISORDERS

Our ongoing research and implementation of our Restorative Medicine Program with scores of patients have continued to demonstrate the overwhelming effectiveness of this approach in treating some of the most common and serious health issues in today's world. In this chapter, we look at some of the issues not covered in previous chapters for which our Restorative Medicine Program is proving successful as we continue to gather more supporting evidence. However, that is not to say that the evidence collected thus far is not impressive: it is. It also involves some of the most insidious health problems affecting Americans today: namely, alcoholism, cancer, gastrointestinal disorders, hair loss, and insomnia. We start our discussion with alcoholism.

Alcoholism

Alcoholism is one of the most pervasive and insidious diseases in our society. According to the National Institute on Alcohol Abuse and Alcoholism, about 17.6 million adults in the United States are alcoholics or have an alcohol problem. Although drinking alcohol under age 21 is illegal, 11 percent of all the alcohol consumed in the United States is by people aged 12 to

20 years, and more than 90 percent of the alcohol these young people consume is done so during binge drinking.

The disease of alcoholism is characterized by four features:

- A strong need/craving to drink

- An inability to stop drinking once you've begun

- Experiencing withdrawal symptoms (e.g., nausea, tremors, sweating) once someone stops drinking

- Tolerance, the need to drink greater amounts of alcohol to get "high"

Alcoholism places people at great risk of liver damage, cognitive dysfunction, certain cancers, birth defects, and death from vehicle accidents and other injuries. It is also a significant drain on our health care system, family and personal relationships, and the workplace.

Causes of Alcoholism

Conventional medicine has proposed several possible causes of alcoholism, including genetic factors that may cause people to be vulnerable to alcoholism and other addictions; presence of high stress and/or anxiety; depression or low self-esteem; and social and/or cultural pressures.

Our research and experience with patients indicates that hormones play a crucial role in alcoholism, and that restoration of hormone balance is key to eliminating this disease. Here is why we believe this.

Hormones and Alcoholism

Numerous studies show the relationship between hormones and alcoholism and other addictive behaviors. For example, we do not believe it is a coincidence that low total cholesterol levels (<160 mg/dL) are seen in men who are heavy drinkers, children who are involved with alcohol and/or substance abuse, and heroin addicts. Because cholesterol is at the top of the hormone cascade (see chart in Chapter 2), we can follow the relationship between alcoholism and the individual hormones in the cascade.

Serotonin and Alcohol

In 2001, scientists from several institutions published (*Journal of Neuroscience*) the results of their research, which demonstrated that drugs of abuse—alcohol, cocaine, and amphetamines—significantly increase the levels of one of the brain's natural painkillers and "feel good" hormones, beta endorphin, in a key part of the brain that influences addiction. It was the first study to show that drugs of abuse increase beta endorphin levels in the nucleus accumbens, the area of the forebrain associated with addictive behavior. This discovery opened the door to possible ways to prevent and treat addictions such as alcoholism.

Where does hormone restoration come into this picture? Several studies show that serotonin (also a "feel good" hormone) may modulate the level of beta-endorphins in the brain. Therefore, we believe that restoration of serotonin and other critical hormones to optimal levels can effectively elevate beta endorphin levels and help quell cravings for alcohol and other drugs of abuse.

Testosterone and Alcohol

Alcohol (ethanol) can cause low sperm counts and impaired sperm motility. Studies of alcoholic men show that they frequently have a significantly low testosterone level, as well as low levels of luteinizing hormone and follicle stimulating hormone. These levels tend to continue to decline the longer they abuse alcohol, throwing the body into further imbalance.

Although low testosterone is often seen in alcoholics, sometimes we see the opposite: elevated levels. A combination of abnormally high serum testosterone and low levels of cortisol have been noted in some male alcoholics who exhibit aggressive, abusive, and/or suicidal behaviors. These behaviors were documented in a Swedish study of 49 male alcoholics, who had either physically abused someone on one or more occasions or who had attempted suicide at least once. The researchers propose that these alcoholics are a subgroup of alcohol abusers who display these characteristics because of hormone imbalances, a genetic predisposition to alcoholism, and certain personality traits.

DHEA and Alcohol

A study conducted by the National Institute on Alcohol Abuse and Alcoholism noted the importance of the DHEA-to-cortisol ratio among abstinent alcoholics, and that an imbalance in this critical ratio (which could be corrected by hormone restoration) increases the risk of relapse. You may recall in an earlier chapter where we noted that a balanced DHEA:cortisol ratio is important for optimal functioning of the adrenal glands. People who abuse alcohol often have adrenal fatigue, in which cortisol output is compromised, which in turn causes an imbalance in the DHEA: cortisol ratio.

Estradiol and Alcohol

In addition to low levels of testosterone, men who abuse alcohol often also have elevated levels of estradiol. In animal studies, rats fed alcohol showed a significant decline in testosterone levels, accompanied by a subsequent significant increase in estrogen (estradiol) levels. The research indicates that alcohol first causes a profound reduction in serum testosterone, which leads to a loss of estrogen-metabolizing enzyme activity and activity of androgen receptors, and a subsequent rise in estradiol. In men, this imbalance often results in feminization, including loss of body hair and enlarged breasts (gynecomastia).

Alcoholism and the HPA Axis

A significant study was conducted at the University of Parma, where investigators studied alcoholics during the early stages of recovery. They found that alcoholics experience dysfunction of the hypothalamic-pituitary-adrenal (HPA) axis, which we discussed in Chapter 2. To refresh your memory, the HPA axis is a system of interactions between the hypothalamus, pituitary gland, and adrenal glands that help regulate the immune system, mood, and other functions. Thus a deficit makes it very difficult for alcoholics to handle psychological and physical stress for about the first eight weeks of abstinence, after which the function of the HPA axis returns to normal.

Specifically, the researchers noted that the secretion of the stress hormones cortisol and adrenocorticotropic hormone (ACTH) were reduced when the men were exposed to stressful situations after four, six, and eight weeks of abstinence, making it difficult for them to cope with the stress. However, the level of these hormones gradually increased over the eight-week period, and at the end, hormone levels returned to normal.

This is not the only study in which dysfunction of the HPA axis has been found to be a key element in alcoholism. In a 2005 Canadian study, investigators explored the idea that individuals who have a family history of alcoholism have a dysfunctional HPA axis that occurs before alcoholism develops. To test this hypothesis, they evaluated the secretions of ACTH, cortisol, and beta-endorphin in blood samples collected every 30 minutes over 24 hours from men who had a family history of alcoholism (high-risk subjects) and those who did not (low-risk subjects). They found that high-risk participants had lower concentrations and lower average values for beta-endorphin and ACTH, but not for cortisol. This finding suggests that a dysfunctional HPA axis can be identified before alcoholism develops in people who are at high risk of the disease, and a dissociation between ACTH and cortisol levels as a function of a family history of alcoholism.

An important review (2006) from scientists at the University of North Carolina School of Medicine, Chapel Hill, notes that activation of the HPA axis results in a rise in gamma-aminobutyric acid (GABA)-ergic neuroactive steroids (e.g., pregnenolone, DHEA, DHEA-S, progesterone) that enhance the transmission of GABA (a "feel good" hormone) and restore homeostatis following stress. This regulation of the HPA axis helps maintain healthy brain function and protects against neuropsychiatric disease. Elevated neuroactive steroids that enhance the effects of GABA on alcohol (ethanol) may prevent excessive drinking behavior, while the lack of neurosteroid responses to alcohol may increase the risk of alcohol abuse. The researchers concluded that neurosteroids may be therapeutic in alcohol withdrawal or to prevent relapse.

We agree, and go a step further, emphasizing the necessity of restoring all the steroidal hormones to optimal levels. This is what we did for Arnold, whose story is below, with excellent results.

Arnold's Story

Arnold, a thirty-eight-year-old auto parts store manager, first contacted us in early 2006. At that time he was 200 pounds (at 6'1"), had a history of attention deficit disorder, was an alcoholic, and abused Xanax, an anti-anxiety drug. He was experiencing memory problems, fatigue, sleep disturbances, and was concerned about being able to keep his job. He agreed to undergo lipid and hormone testing, and the results were as follows:

Hormone	Reference Range	2006	2008
Total Cholesterol	< 200 mg/dL	229 mg/dL	209 mg/dL
Total Testosterone	241-827 ng/dL	543 ng/dL	564 ng/dL
DHEA-S	280-640 ug/dL	324 ug/dL	642 ug/dL
Pregnenolone	10-200 ng/dL	33 ng/dL	95 ng/dL
Cortisol	4.3-22.4 ug/dL	9.2 ug/dL	Not Taken

We started Arnold on a program of hormone restoration and nutrients. Over a two-year period, Arnold contacted us several times to let us know how he was doing. We were happy to learn that Arnold had completely stopped drinking six months after starting the Program and has had no urge to do so. Because he did not want to undergo follow-up blood testing, we made some adjustments to his Program based on his reports. He did agree to have a blood test in 2008, and the results are shown here.

Since that time, he has refused to be retested, but he has told us that he continues to be free of alcohol and any urge to drink or abuse drugs. He also says he has "tons of energy," he's down to 185 pounds, and greatly enjoys spending time at the gym.

Cancer

In the fight against cancer, regardless of the part of the body that is affected, one of the best defenses you can have is a strong immune system. Research shows that the immune system plays a major role in protecting the body against the development of cancer and in helping fight cancer if it is already present. An immune system that has been compromised by aging, poor nutrition or environmental factors such as smoke or pesticide exposure, among other factors, is susceptible to cancerous growth. Evidence indicates that many people with cancer have slowed progression of the disease and thus extended their life and improved its quality when they enhanced their immune system. Our Restorative Medicine Program can be helpful in taking on the challenge of cancer, because it incorporates optimal hormonal balance, which strengthens the immune system.

That is not to say that hormonal restorative therapy is a cure for cancer; it is not. But we have found that bringing hormones back into balance, along with the use of selected antioxidants and substances that block the activity of immunosuppressive factors, can have very impressive results.

Our Restorative Medicine Program's Effects on the Immune System

As we mentioned at the beginning of this section on cancer, strengthening the immune system is critical in order to defend against cancer and improve quality of life for cancer patients. For these patients, our Restorative Medicine Program places extra emphasis on the immune system, and it includes the use of steroid hormones, along with antioxidants and a few suppressive agents, which work together at several levels to strengthen the immune system. Immunotherapy is a type of biological therapy, in which natural body substances (e.g., bio-identical hormones) and/or drugs made from natural body substances are used to treat cancer and especially boost the immune system. Immunotherapy can be helpful in treating cancer because cancer cells are abnormal, and so they are picked up by the immune system.

Before we can talk about how hormones and other compounds boost the immune system, there are some things you need to know about how the major players in the immune system work.

Immune System Players

One of those key players is the macrophage, which is a type of white blood cell that ingests foreign materials and helps destroy tumor cells, bacteria, and protozoa. Macrophages also release substances that stimulate other cells of the immune system. Thus, one of the goals of our Restorative Medicine Program is to stimulate recognition of cancer cells by macrophages.

Another immune system factor is natural killer cells. These cells hone in on their targets—tumor cells or various infectious microorganisms—and kill on contact. Their function is influenced by growth hormone and luteinizing hormone.

Growth hormone is important in cancer patients because it increases strength and lean body mass.

Other immune system factors that we need to consider include T-cells, B-cells, and interleukin-2 (IL-2). T-cells, so-called because they mature in the thymus gland, are white blood cells (lymphocytes) that destroy certain types of invaders in the immune system. Also known as T lymphocytes, these cells can produce substances called cytokines, such as the interleukins, which further stimulate the immune system response.

B-cells (B lymphocytes), which mature in bone marrow, make proteins called antibodies that fight against bacteria and viruses. Antibodies have two ends: one end, called the variable end, sticks to damaged cells and helps to kill them. Some antibodies with variable ends that recognize cancer cells adhere to them and destroy them.

Interleukin-2 is a chemical that boosts the immune system's response to help destroy cancer cells.

Now that you better understand some of the immune system factors that are important in cancer, what impact does our Restorative Medicine Program have on them?

How our Restorative Medicine Program Impacts the Immune System Players

The hormones used in our Restorative Medicine Program have a positive impact on the immune system. Estrogens and DHEA stimulate the macrophages to recognize cancer cells so they can be destroyed. Estrogen, along with other steroid hormones, also increases the production of growth hormone. DHEA stimulates T-cells and B-cells and regulates production of IL-2. Testosterone causes the secretion of hormones from the thymus, called humoral factors, which improves function of T-cells. The antioxidants Vitamins C and E, and the mineral selenium are administered to boost the immune system as well.

One of the few medications that we recommend is bromocriptine (Parlodel), a drug that blocks the release of a hormone called prolactin, which is secreted by the pituitary gland. Prolactin affects menstruation and is used to treat infertility that is caused by excess prolactin production in both women and men. Bromocriptine also stimulates production of growth hormone, increases natural killer cell counts, and improves stamina and strength.

Another medication that is helpful is cimetidine, which is a common over-the-counter drug used to treat heartburn and indigestion. Research conducted over the past few decades indicates that cimetidine can be used to treat cancer. Cancer is associated with excessive levels and/or activity of suppressor T-cells. Cimetidine can block activity of these cells.

Hormones and Prostate Cancer

One of the questions that invariably arises whenever we talk to people about using hormones is whether their use can result in the development of cancer. Many people, for example, are concerned about a link between testosterone and the development of prostate cancer (see "Jim's Story" below). In fact, the opposite appears to be true: men who have high levels of testosterone tend to have less aggressive prostate cancer and live longer, and low levels of testosterone may actually be linked with a greater risk of the disease.

The whole idea that testosterone causes prostate cancer began in the 1940s when Charles B. Huggins, a urologist from the University of Chicago, was studying benign enlargement of the prostate gland, also known as benign prostatic hyperplasia (BPH). He discovered that when he performed castration on dogs that had BPH, not only did the prostate shrink, but areas that looked like human prostate cancer in the dogs also disappeared. Since it was known that castration reduces testosterone levels in the blood, Huggins decided to lower the testosterone levels in men who had prostate cancer that had spread to their bones. He used two different methods: castration and estrogen injections.

Through a series of experiments, including those in which he used the two above-named techniques and ones in which he injected testosterone into men with prostate cancer, Huggins and his colleagues concluded that lowering testosterone levels reduced prostate cancer, and raising the hormone level caused its growth. Neither castration nor estrogen treatment (which caused blood clots and heart attacks in some men) were popular ways to deal with BPH, so the introduction in the 1980s of a new type of medication called LHRH agonists was welcomed. Use of LHRH agonists is now the most commonly used way to lower testosterone in men who have prostate cancer, among physicians who still believe that testosterone plays a role in causing the disease.

Testosterone Does Not Cause Prostate Cancer

Why did Huggins' work seem to show that testosterone caused prostate cancer? Because his work did not go far enough. Perhaps the most convincing research available thus far was published in the *Journal of the National Cancer Institute* in 2008. The report was conducted by the Endogenous Hormones and Prostate Cancer Collaborative Group and the investigators collected data from 18 prospective studies that included 3,886 men with prostate cancer and 6,438 controls. The experts concluded that there was no association between the risk of prostate cancer and concentrations of testosterone, free testosterone, dihydrotestosterone (DHT), DHEA, androstenedione, estradiol, or free estradiol.

Other dedicated scientists have shown that when testosterone levels in the blood are raised, they do not rise within the prostate. If a man is taking testosterone supplementation, once the prostate has been exposed to a sufficient amount of the hormone, any "leftover" testosterone is treated as excess and does not build up in the prostate gland. In other words, the prostate reaches a saturation point when it comes to testosterone. Experimental studies indicate that the concentration at which saturation occurs is quite low.

Abraham Morgentaler, MD, a urologist at Harvard Medical School and author of *Testosterone For Life: Recharge*

Your Sex Drive, Muscle Mass, Energy and Overall Health, adds the following conclusions based on his work, which highlights the main points:

- Low levels of testosterone in the bloodstream do not protect against prostate cancer, and they may in fact increase the risk

- High levels of testosterone in the blood do not increase the risk of prostate cancer

- Use of testosterone treatment does not increase the risk of prostate cancer, even among men who are already at high risk for the disease

Jim's Story

Jim is a 64-year-old engineer who has a history of chronic lymphocytic leukemia, coronary artery disease, and an elevated PSA level. During his first visit with us in 2004, he explained that he took 2 to 4 nitroglycerin tablets daily for angina. Jim had had previous stent surgery, but his cardiologists had told him that he was not a good candidate for additional stent surgery nor bypass surgery because he had too many blockages. Given his leukemia and heart condition, his prognosis, according to his doctors, was a maximum of one to two years. At the time, Jim said he was always tired, experienced mental "fogginess," had erectile dysfunction, and felt "like I'm ninety-five years old." He was taking multiple medications for coronary artery disease and leukemia. He agreed to undergo testing for hormone and lipid levels, and the results revealed significant deficiencies in pregnenolone,

DHEA-S, testosterone, and progesterone. We immediately started him on our Restorative Medicine Program.

Jim continued with the Program that we developed for him and defied the prediction of his physicians. When he last contacted us in late 2008, he said, "I feel fantastic." His chronic lymphocytic leukemia had improved significantly: his white blood count dropped from 40,000 to 18,000. Although this is not considered a cure, restoration of Jim's hormone levels and administration of other supplementation clearly made a difference by improving his quality of life and prolonging it as well.

Jim's heart function had also improved so much that he no longer needs nitroglycerine for angina. We would also like to note that despite warnings and protests from his family and general practitioner that use of testosterone would lead to prostate cancer, Jim agreed to include testosterone restoration as part of his Program. After more than four years since starting treatment, Jim's PSA count has remained stable and he has no signs of prostate cancer.

Hair Loss

Hair loss is a physical condition that is the source of much emotional distress among both men and women. Although there are several types of hair loss that affect both sexes, the most common type in general is androgenetic alopecia, which is male- and female-pattern baldness. Approximately 65 million men and 25 million women experience hair loss in the

United States. Because hair loss in men is more common, that is the focus of our discussion. However, our approach to treatment for hair loss in both men and women is the same—restoration of hormone and nutrient balance.

Men who are losing their hair and who want to stop hair loss sometimes turn to a prescription medication called Propecia. One problem with Propecia, however, is that it can cause erectile dysfunction. The reason for the tradeoff—hair growth but lost erections—is that the drug blocks the conversion of testosterone to dihydrotestosterone, the testosterone derivative that causes hair loss.

Yet as an aside, we had noticed that none of our patients who were taking testosterone were experiencing hair loss. In fact, their hair was growing better than it had before they started their treatment program. At first, this didn't make sense to us: if patients were taking testosterone, then their levels were rising and there was more hormone to convert to dihydrotestosterone, which causes hair to fall out. Then we remembered the fact that made the difference: dihydrotestosterone is much more powerful than testosterone. Therefore, here's our hypothesis to explain the apparent paradox:

When testosterone levels in the body decline, the body converts what's left of the hormone to dihydrotestosterone because DHT is more powerful, and a little goes a long way. However, the body has to pay a price for this conversion, and that price is hair loss and, in some men, an enlarged prostate.

Therefore, to avoid forcing the body to optimize the low amount of testosterone that it has, we restore testosterone levels to optimal levels, so no conversion needs to occur. For extra protection, we typically recommend certain supplements that block the conversion to DHT, such as zinc and saw palmetto.

Although we can truthfully say that no one has come to us with hair loss as his or her main complaint, neither have any of our clients complained about the added bonus of better hair growth. The ability of hormone restoration to effectively treat this common condition is just one more example of the "one disease, one treatment" approach that works so well.

Insomnia

Claudia has been on a fast track for months. She gets up at 5 AM, straightens up the house, gets her two elementary school children off to school, works from 9 until 3, helps her children with their homework, prepares dinner, attends college classes three nights a week, studies until midnight or until she falls asleep, exhausted, and starts all over again the next morning. Except that lately she doesn't stay asleep. She's tosses and turns, falls asleep but can't stay asleep. One night she dozed off while driving home from class and nearly hit a tree. She knew her sleepless nights had become a big problem.

Insomnia is a sleep disorder in which people have difficulty falling or staying asleep, or the sleep they do get does not leave them feeling refreshed or restored. Insomnia is considered to be chronic if these difficulties occur most nights, and lasts a month or longer.

Insomnia: More than Lack of Sleep

Insomnia is a major problem for several reasons. One obvious reason is that the body needs restorative sleep, and insomnia robs you of it. Adults generally need seven to eight hours of sleep per night. When people try to function on less, especially on a regular basis, their physical, emotional, and mental health suffers. We know, for example, that sleep deprivation causes elevated levels of C-reaction protein, a marker of inflammation that is strongly associated with risk of cardiovascular disease.

Lack of sleep also causes elevated levels of the stress hormone cortisol and disrupts glucose control, a major factor in diabetes. Studies also show that adults who sleep less than seven hours a night have a significantly higher risk of obesity, which may be associated with hormone imbalance. Insufficient sleep also affects cognition and memory, and may be a factor in chronic fatigue syndrome, fibromyalgia, and migraine. People who have insomnia are more likely to experience emotional and psychological problems, require hospitalization, and are at greater risk of dying than people who get sufficient sleep.

Cancer also has been linked to lack of sleep and shift work. That's because melatonin, which is normally produced at night, may modulate the relationship between shift work and cancer. Some research indicates that melatonin has cancer-preventive potential, and if a person has low levels of melatonin because they are exposed to light at night, which hinders the production of melatonin, there may be a tendency for tumor development. Clearly insomnia is not a benign condition.

Causes of Insomnia

Insomnia can be caused by a long list of physical, psychological, lifestyle, pharmaceutical, and environmental factors, and in many people more than one factor contributes to their chronic inability to get sufficient sleep. Physical conditions and illnesses such as heart disease, digestive problems (ulcers, heartburn, gastroesophageal reflux), allergies, arthritis, cancer, fibromyalgia, sleep apnea, restless leg syndrome, hot flashes, and asthma, among other ailments, can cause insomnia. Depression, anxiety, attention deficit hyperactivity disorder, and bipolar disorder are causes as well. In fact, more than 90 percent of depressed individuals experience insomnia.

Taking medication is such a common part of our society that most people don't think twice about some of the side effects they can cause. Antidepressants, corticosteroids, diuretics, histamine blockers, respiratory stimulants, antihypertensive drugs, and drugs used to treat asthma can all cause insomnia. Disruptive lifestyle habits, such as poor nutrition, lack of exercise, excessive intake of caffeine, drinking alcohol, smoking, and use if illicit drugs can cause insomnia. Environmental factors, such as noise, light (especially at night), heat, cold, and irritating pollutants are other considerations.

The hormones melatonin, serotonin, cortisol, and growth hormone all play a role in sleep and insomnia. As we have discussed previously, melatonin is a key component of the sleep/wake cycle. Thus, the fact that people with chronic insomnia often have low levels of melatonin and high levels of cortisol is not surprising. Growth hormone is associated with deep sleep, and its levels decline with age, which can contribute to insomnia, especially among older adults.

Treating Insomnia

In our society, the most common treatment for insomnia is sleeping pills, which does nothing to address the cause of the sleeplessness. In fact, in some people, use of sleep medication exacerbates insomnia. If lifestyle changes, use of medications, and/or modifiable environmental factors are not helpful, or even if they are but they do not eliminate the insomnia, then hormone restoration is recommended. Our experience has been that the majority of patients who have participated in our Restorative Medicine Program and who had insomnia as a symptom have been relieved of this problem. Regardless of the accompanying health condition, we have successfully treated insomnia using hormones and nutritional supplements.

Because melatonin is the hormone that regulates the body's biological clock, and levels of this hormone are often out of balance, we include melatonin supplements as part of our Program. Other supplements that we typically recommend include kava root extract (for anxiety and muscle relaxation; up to three months of use only), B vitamins (for stress reduction), and magnesium (promotes calm). Other supplements that have proven effective for many people include S-adenosylmethionine (SAMe; a substance produced naturally by the body, inositol (a member of the B vitamin family), and omega-3 fatty acids, all of which can help insomnia related to mood disorders. Herbs that have a calming effect include lavender and lemon balm (as essential oils, for external use only in aromatherapy applications), chamomile (as a tea or extract; avoid if you have ragweed or related allergies), and valerian (400-500 mg taken 30 minutes before bedtime is usually effective).

Other ways to help prevent and treat insomnia include:

- Avoid using caffeine, nicotine, alcohol, and stimulating drugs late in the day, if you use them. Eliminating them from your lifestyle is best.

- If you use prescription medications that may be stimulating, take them as long before bedtime as you can.

- Avoid eating a large meal in the evening.

- Get regular exercise, but avoid vigorous physical activity near bedtime.

- Adopt stress-reducing practices, such as meditation, listening to soothing music, yoga, or a warm bath.

- Avoid taking naps during the day. If you really need one, take just one 20-minute nap.

- Keep your sleep environment as pleasant and stress-free as possible. Bed clothes, linens, pillows, room temperature, and noise levels should be comfortable.

Gastrointestinal Disorders

Have you ever wondered why we use expressions like "follow your gut" and "gut instinct?" These sayings are more than mere whimsy; they point to a biological phenomenon known as the brain-gut axis. The brain-gut axis is a network characterized by a continuous, rapid exchange of electrical and chemical signals that occurs between the central nervous system (brain) and the digestive system (gut). Some experts even refer to the gut as the "second brain," and here's why.

The brain and the gut both are home to the some of the same substances, including the neurotransmitter serotonin. You may know serotonin as the chemical in the brain that plays a major role in mood. However, you may be surprised to learn that 95 percent of the serotonin in the body actually resides in the gut, a fact that strongly supports the intimate connection between the brain and the gut. Other important chemicals that the brain and gut share include dopamine, norepinephrine, and nitric oxide, along with various brain proteins. Yet another connection between the brain and gut is the vagus nerve.

Vagus Nerve

The vagus nerve, which runs from the brain stem through organs in the neck, thorax, and abdomen, is the main pathway for the electrical and chemical signals that travel between the brain and gut. Some of the communication that passes between these two areas of the body includes signals associated with acetylcholine and adrenaline, which let the stomach know when to start and stop producing acid. These substances also signal the intestines as to when they should move their contents. Messages also travel from the digestive system to the brain, and these signals can result in nausea, hunger, pain, and fullness. Messages from the gut to the brain can also affect mood, leading to depression, and contribute to hormone imbalances.

Gastrointestinal Disorders, Probiotics and Restorative Hormones

Another critical part of restoring balance to the gastrointestinal system is the use of probiotics. Probiotics are "good" or "beneficial" bacteria that reside in the gastrointestinal system alongside "bad" bacteria. The nonbeneficial bacteria are responsible for, or are key players in conditions such as irritable bowel, constipation, inflammatory bowel disease, malnutrition and acid reflux, among others. Our goal in administering probiotics is to restore a healthy balance to the bacterial flora in the gut. We have found that this step, along with hormone restoration, is effective in eliminating gastrointestinal conditions.

The most common and effective probiotics are the *Bifidobacteria, Streptococcus and Lactobacilli* species. These bacteria are capable of the following functions:

- Assist in the absorption of nutrients into the bloodstream.

- Form a protective barrier against bad bacteria that can cause diarrhea

- Manufacture food for the intestinal tract cells so they can function optimally.

- Help prevent harmful bacteria from causing damage to the intestinal tract

- In some cases, probiotics produce natural antibiotics that destroy harmful bacteria, viruses, fungi and yeasts.

- Prevent symptoms caused by use of antibiotics, which can destroy most of the good bacteria in the intestinal tract

Connie's Story

To give an example of how probiotics can help eliminate gastrointestinal disorders, as well as restorative hormones, we can look at Connie's story. Like all of our patients, she came to use with many complaints, including migraine, depression, fibromyalgia and severe constipation. Migraine and gastrointestinal problems are a very common combination; in fact, 70 percent of migraineurs have some type of gastrointestinal disorder. So when Connie, a 50-year-old former retail store manager, came to see us, we were confident from past experience that along with eliminating migraine, we could also relieve her of the persistent constipation and other complaints if she followed the program.

In the early 1980s, Connie, a trim 130 pounds at five-foot-six, developed back pain that was followed within several months by migraine, persistent constipation, insomnia, severe fatigue, stiff joints and panic attacks. Her weight quickly ballooned to 170 pounds and her periods stopped completely, along with her libido. She was thoroughly confused by these events and sought help from several specialists, who told her that her symptoms were "her imagination" and the result of stress. She was prescribed multiple medications, and also tried various therapies, including acupuncture, water exercise therapy, massage and chiropractic adjustments, but she got little satisfaction.

In 2000, Connie was diagnosed with fibromyalgia by a rheumatologist, and although she was relieved that a medical professional had finally believed that she was "really" ill, she was also discouraged because "I had already tried so many different drugs and therapies that are typically recommended for fibromyalgia and none of them had worked." She became depressed and developed insomnia.

By the time Connie came to see us, she was taking multiple medications, including bupropion (Wellbutrin®, an antidepressant), clonazepam (Klonopin®, an anticonvulsant used for depression), zoldipem (Ambien®, for insomnia) and synthetic hormone replacement therapy, as well as several pain killers. After we reviewed her personal and family medical history, we determined that her symptoms were related to hormonal imbalance, and recommended that she have her hormone levels checked.

Connie agreed, and when her results came back, we started her on our Restorative Medicine Program. Within one month of starting treatment, Connie reported that her migraines were nearly gone, and that her fibromyalgia pain, depression and sleep had all improved. In fact, she felt well enough to stop taking both antidepressants, and to wean herself off the insomnia medication. Her constipation, however, continued to be a problem. This was understandable, given the severity of the problem, the length of time she had suffered with I, and the large number of medications she had been taking for so many years. This last fact was significant because prolonged use of drugs, whether they are prescription or over-the-counter, can greatly compromise the intestinal flora, resulting in an excess of "bad" bacteria.

Part of her original treatment Program had included probiotics. We recommended that she increase her daily intake of probiotics from one scoop to two scoops daily (one in the morning and one at night), as well as use a one-month parasite-cleansing program that contained herbs, fiber and fructooligosaccharides (FOS). FOS are nondigestible fibers that are often recommended for people who have gastrointestinal disorders because they promote the health of friendly bacteria in the gut. We also suggested she add two scoops of magnesium citrate supplement daily, because magnesium deficiency is associated with gastrointestinal disorders. In terms of her diet, we suggested that she significantly reduce her use of dietary sugar, because it promotes the growth of bad bacteria.

Within one month, Connie's constipation had resolved and she was completely free of her insomnia medication. Four months after she started treatment, Connie reported that "I never would have believed I could feel this good again." Today Connie is free of constipation, fibromyalgia, migraine, depression, pain and sleep problems. She has lost weight, is medication-free and continues with a modified hormone therapy Program, along with several nutritional supplements, including probiotics as needed.

References

Chapter 1

Beers MH, et al. The Merck Manual, 18th ed. Merck, 2006.

De Bree A, et al. Homocysteine determinants and the evidence to what extent homocysteine determines the risk of coronary heart disease. Pharmacol Rev 2002 Dec;54(4):599-618.

Fauci AS, et al. Harrison's Principles of Internal Medicine, 17th ed. New York: McGraw-Hill Professional, 2008.

Kellogg JH. The Battle Creek Sanitarium System: History, Organization, Methods. Gage Printing Co., 1908.

Chapter 2

Ahmed MH, Osman MM, Alokail MS. Statins and breast cancer: a smoking gun or guilt by association? Expert Opin Drug Saf 2006 Sep;5(5):599-601.

American Heart Association. Statistics on high blood pressure, at http://www.americanheart.org/presenter.jhtml?identifier=4621

Borrego FJ, et al. Rhabdomyolysis and acute renal failure secondary to statins. Nefrologia 2001 May-Jun;21(3):309-13.

Boston PF, Dursun SM, Reveley MA. Cholesterol and mental disorder. Br J Psychiatry 1996 Dec;169(6):682-9.

Chopra D, et al. 'Alternative' medicine is mainstream. Wall Street Journal 2009 Jan 9; http://online.wsj.com/article/SB123146318996466585.html?mod=djemITP

Deedwania P, et al. Reduction of low-density lipoprotein cholesterol in patients with coronary heart disease and metabolic syndrome: analysis of the Treating to New Targets study. Lancet 2006;368:919-28.

Gaist D, et al. Statins and risk of polyneuropathy: a case-control study. Neurology 2002 May 14;58(9):1333-7.

Gaist D, et al. Are users of lipid-lowering drugs at increased risk of peripheral neuropathy? Eur J Clin Pharmacol 2001 Mar;56(12):931-3.

Goldstein MR, Mascitelli L. Do statins decrease cardiovascular disease at the expense of increasing cancer? Int J Cardiol 2009 Apr 3;133(2):254-5. Epub 2007 Dec 31.

Golomb BA, Kane T, Dimsdale JE. Severe irritability associated with statin cholesterol-lowering drugs. QJM 2004 Apr;97(4):229-35.

Hall SA, et al. Do statins affect androgen levels in men? Results from the Boston area community health survey. Cancer Epidemiol Biomarkers Prev 2007 Aug;16(8):1587-94.

Horlitz M, Sigwart U, Niebauer J. Statins do not prevent restenosis after coronary angioplasty: where to go from here? Herz 2001 Mar;26(2):119-28.

Jackson AA. Human nutrition in medical practice: the training of doctors. Proc Nutr Soc 2001;60:257-63.

Jacquet A, et al. A one-year prospective and intensive pharmacovigilance of antilipemic drugs in an hospital consultation for prevention of risk factors. Therapie 1993 Sep-Oct;48(5):509-12.

Krebs NF, Primak LE. Comprehensive integration of nutrition into medical training. Am J Clin Nutr 2006 Apr;83(4):945S-50S.

Law MR, Thompson SG, Wakd NJ. Assessing possible hazards of reducing serum cholesterol. BMJ 1994 Feb 5;308(6925):373-9.

Manzoli A, et al. Statins: from hypocholesteremic drugs to antiatherogenic agents. Clin Ther 2001 Sep-Oct;152(5):307-13.

National Center for Health Statistics website, accessed 2/2/09: http://www.cdc.gov/nchs/fastats/exercise.htm

Newman TB, Hulley SB. Carcinogenicity of lipid-lowering drugs. JAMA. 1996 Jan 3;275(1):55-60.

Ormiston T, et al. Hormonal changes with cholesterol reduction: a double-blind pilot study. J Clin Pharm Ther 2004 Feb;29(1):71-3.

Pignone M, Phillips C, Mulrow C. Use of lipid lowering drugs for primary prevention of coronary heart disease: meta-analysis of randomised trials. BMJ 2000 Oct 21;321(7267):983-6.

Rizvi K, Hampson JP, Harvey JN. Do lipid-lowering drugs cause erectile dysfunction? A systematic review. Fam Pract 2002 Feb;19(1):95-8.

Rosengren A, et al, for the INTERHEART investigators. Association of psychosocial risk factors with risk of acute myocardial infarction in 11,119 cases and 13,648 controls from 52 countries (the INTERHEART study): case-control study. Lancet 2004;364:953-62.

Scheen AJ. Fatal rhabdomyolysis caused by cerivastatin. Rev Med Liege 2001 Aug;56(8):592-4.

Schuff-Werner P, Kohlschein P. Current therapy of hypercholesterolemia. How much statin does your patient need? MMW Fortschr Med 2002 Aug 8;144(31-32):24-6.

Sirvent P, Mercier J, Lacampagne A. New insights into mechanisms of statin-associated myotoxicity. Curr Opin Pharmacol 2008 Jun;8(3):333-8. Epub 2008 Feb 1.

Tiwari A, et al. Statins and myotoxicity: a therapeutic limitation. Expert Opin Drug Saf 2006 Sep;5(5):651-66.

Tomlinson B, Chan P, Lan W. How well tolerated are lipid-lowering drugs? Drugs Aging 2001;18(9):665-83.

US patients suffer more medical errors, published on line on November 13, 2008 at www.UPI.com

Yusuf S et al, on behalf of the INTERHEART Study Investigators. Effect of potentially modifiable risk factors associated with myocardial infarction in 52 countries (the INTERHEART study): case-control study. Lancet 2004;364:937-52.

Chapter 3

Barrett-Connor E, Goodman-Gruen D. The epidemiology of DHEAS and cardiovascular disease. Ann NY Acad Sci 1995 Dec 29;774:259-70.

Buvat J. Androgen therapy with dehydroepiandrosterone. World J Urol 2003 Nov;21(5):346-55.

Dzugan SA, Smith RA. Hypercholesterolemia treatment: a new hypothesis or just an accident? Med Hypotheses 2002 Dec;59(6):751-6.

Ferrari E, et al. Age-related changes of the hypothalamic-pituitary-adrenal axis: pathophysiological correlates. Eur J Endocrinol 2001 Apr;144(4):319-29.

Kalmijn S, et al. A prospective study on cortisol, dehydroepiandrosterone sulfate, and cognitive function in the elderly. J Clin Endocrinol Metab 1998 Oct;83(10):3487-92.

Laughlin GA, Barrett-Connor E. Sexual dimorphismin the influence of advanced aging on adrenal hormone levels: the Rancho Bernardo Study. J Clin Endocrinol Metab 2000 Oct;85(1):3561-8.

Lubet RA, et al. Modulation of methylnitrosourea-induced breast cancer in Sprague Dawley rats by dehydroepiandrosterone: dose-dependent inhibition, effects of limited exposure, effects on peroxisomal enzymes, and lack of effects on levels of Ha-Ras mutations. Cancer Res 1998 Mar 1;59(5):921-6.

McGavack TH, Chevalley J, Weissberg J. The use of delta 5-pregnenolone in various clinical disorders. J Clin Endocrinol Metab 1951 Jun;11(6):559-77.

Mayo W, et al. Pregnenolone sulfate enhances neurogenesis and PSA-NCAM in young and aged hippocampus. Neurobiol Aging 2005 Jan;26(1):103-14.

Moore MA, et al. Modifying influence of dehydroepiandrosterone on the development of dihydroxy-di-n-propylnitrosamine-initiated lesions in the thyroid, lung and liver of F344 rats. Carcinogenesis 1986 Feb;7(2):311-6.

Pelissier MA, et al. Antioxidant effects of dehydroepiandrosterone and 7alpha-hydroxy-dehydroepiandrosterone in the rat colon, intestine and liver. Steroids 2004 Feb;69(2):137-44.

Roberts E. Pregnenolone—from Selye to Alzheimer and a model of the pregnenolone sulfate binding site on the GABA receptor. Biochem Pharmacol 1995 Jan 6;49(1):1-16.

Schwartz AG, Pashko LL. Cancer chemoprevention with the adrenocortical steroid dehydroepiandrosterone and structural analogs. J Cell Biochem Suppl 1993;17G:73-9.

Chapter 4

Available at http://www.americanheart.org/presenter.jhtml?identifier=2876 accessed December 3, 2008.

Andersen P, et al. Reduced fibrinolytic capacity associated with low ratio of serum testosterone to oestradiol in healthy coronary high-risk men. Scand J Haematol 1983;30(Suppl 39):53-7.

Anker SD, et al. Hormonal changes and catabolic/anabolic imbalance in chronic heart failure and their importance for cardiac cachexia. Circulation 1997;96:526-34.

Azuma J, et al. Double-blind randomized crossover trial of taurine in congestive heart failure. Curr Ther Res 1983;34(4):543-57.

Azuma J, et al. Therapeutic effect of taurine in congestive heart failure: A double-blind crossover trial. Clin Cardiol 1985;8:276-82.

Baggio E, et al. Italian multicenter study on the safety and efficacy of coenzyme Q10 as adjunctive therapy in heart failure. CoQ10 Drug Surveillance Investigators. Mol Aspects Med 1994;15 Suppl:s287-94.

Bahorun T. Antioxidant activities of Cragaegus monogyna extracts. Planta Medica 1994;60:323-38.

Barrett-Connor E, et al. A prospective study of dehydroepiandrosterone sulfate, mortality, and cardiovascular disease. N Engl J Med 1986;315:1519-24.

Cohen N, et al. Metabolic and clinical effects of oral magnesium supplementation in furosemide-treated patients with severe congestive heart failure. Clin Cardiol 2000;23(6):433-36.

Dzugan SA, Smith AR. Hypercholesterolemia treatment: a new hypothesis or just an accident? Med Hypotheses 2002;59(6):751-6.

Dzugan S. Natural approaches in the treatment of congestive heart failure. Life Extension 2003 Dec;60-8.

Dzugan S. Women and coronary heart disease. A novel approach to coronary heart disease prevention. Life Extension 2005 Aug;50-9.

Ebeling P, Koivisto VA Physiological importance of dehydroepiandrosterone. Lancet 1994 Jun 11;343(8911):1479-81.

English KM, et al. Men with coronary artery disease have lower levels of androgens than men with normal coronary angiograms. Eur Heart J 2000 Jun;21(11):890-4.

Fong HH, Bauman JL. Hawthorn. J Cardiovasc Nurs 2002 Jul;16(4):1-8.

Fugh-Berman A. Herbs and dietary supplements in the prevention and treatment of cardiovascular disease. Prev Cardiol 2000;3(1):24-32.

Gordon GB, et al. Reduction of atherosclerosis by administration of dehydroepiandrosterone. A study in the hypercholesterolemic New Zealand white rabbit with aortic intimal injury. J Clin Invest 1988;82:712-20.

Herrington DM. Dehydroepiandrosterone and coronary atherosclerosis. Ann N Y Acad Sci 1995;774:271-80.

Jones RD, et al. Testosterone and atherosclerosis in aging men: purported association and clinical implications. Am J Cardiovasc Drugs 2005;5(3):141-54.

Kochanek KD, et al. Death: Final data for 2002. National vital statistics reports; vol 53 no 5. Hyattsville, MD: National Center for Health Statistics, 2004.

Kontoleon PE, et al. Hormonal profile in patients with congestive heart failure. Int J Cardiol 2003;87(2-3):179-83.

Labrie F, et al. DHEA and the intracrine formation of androgens and estrogens in peripheral target tissues: its role during aging. Steroids 1998 May;63(5-6):322-8.

Langsjoen PH, Langsjoen AM. Coenzyme Q10 in cardiovascular disease with emphasis on heart failure and myocardial ischemia. Asia Pac Heart J 1998;7:160-8.

Leuchtgens H. Crataegus Special Extract WS 1442 in NYHA II heart failure. A placebo controlled randomized double-blind study. Fortschr Med 1993;111(20-21):352-4.

Mendelsohn ME, Karas RH. The protective effects of estrogen on the cardiovascular system. N Engl J Med 1999 Jun 10;340(23):1801-11.

Pucciarelli G, et al. The clinical and hemodynamic effects of propionyl-L-carnitine in the treatment of congestive heart failure. Clin Ter 1992 Nov;141(11):379-84.

Pugh PJ, et al. Testosterone: a natural tonic for the failing heart? QJM 2000;93(10):689-94.

Schaffer SW, et al. Interaction between the actions of taurine and angiotensin II. Amino Acids 2000;18(4):305-18.

Seelig MS. Interrelationship of magnesium and congestive heart failure Wien Med Wochenschr 2000;150(15-16):335-41.

Sewdarsen M, et al. Sex hormone levels in young Indian patients with myocardial infarction. Arteriosclerosis 1986 Jul-Aug;6(4):418-21.

Tappler B, Katz M. Pituitary-gonadal dysfunction in low-output cardiac failure. Clin Endocrinol 1979;10(3):219-26.

Tripathi Y, Hegde BM. Serum estradiol and testosterone levels following acute myocardial infarction in men. Indian J Physiol Pharmacol 1998 Apr;42(2):291-4.

Vermeulen A. Dehydroepiandrosterone sulfate and aging. Ann NY Acad Sci 1995 Dec 29;774:121-7.

Weikl A, et al. Crataegus Special Extract WS 1442. Assessment of objective effectiveness in patients with heart failure (NYHA II). Fortschr Med 1996 Aug 30;114(24):291-6.

Chapter 5

Atmaca M, et al. Serum leptin and cholesterol levels in patients with bipolar disorder. Neuropsychobiology 2002;46(4):176-9.

Behar S, et al. Low total cholesterol is associated with high total mortality in patients with coronary heart disease. The Bezafibrate Infarction Prevention (BIP) Study Group. Eur Heart J 1997 Jan;18(1):52-9.

Bratus VV, Talaieva TV, et al. Modified lipoproteins – their types and role in atherogenesis. Fiziol Zh 2000;46(2):73-81.

Cassidy F, Carroll BJ. Hypocholesterolemia during mixed manic episodes. Eur Arch Psychiatry Clin Neurosci 2002 Jun;252(3):110-4.

Corti MC, et al. Clarifying the direct relation between total cholesterol levels and death from coronary heart disease in older persons. Ann Intern Med 1997 May 15;126(10):753-60.

Dzugan SA, Smith RA. Broad spectrum restoration in natural steroid hormones as possible treatment for hypercholesterolemia. Bull Urg Rec Med 2002;3(20):278-84.

Dzugan SA, Smith RA. Hypercholesterolemia treatment: a new hypothesis or just an accident. Med Hypothesis 2002;59(6):751-6.

Dzugan SA, Smith RA. Treating high cholesterol by repalcing hormoens lost to aging. Life Extension 2003 Sep;41-8.

Dzugan SA, Smith RA, Kuznetsov AS. A new statin free method of hypercholesterolemia. Health Don 2004;4:19-25.

Goldstein JL, Hazzard WR, Schrott HG, et al. Hyperlipidemia in coronary heart disease. I. Lipid levels in 500 survivors of myocardial infarction. J Clin Invest 1973 Jul;52(7):1533-43.

Hawthon K, et al. Low serum cholesterol and suicide. Br J Psychiatry 1993 Jun;162:818-25.

Iribarren C, et al. Low serum cholesterol and mortality. Which is the cause and which is the effect? Circulation 1995 Nov 1;92(9):2396-403.

Iribarren C, et al. Serum total cholesterol and mortality. Confounding factors and risk modifications in Japanese-American men. JAMA 1995 Jun 28;273(24):1926-32.

Jacobson TA. Clinical context: current concepts of coronary heart disease management. Am J Med 2001;110 Suppl 6A:3S-11S.

Kuhar MB. Update on managing hypercholesterolemia. The new NCEP guidelines. AAOHN J 2002 Aug;50(8):360-4.

Ladeia AM, Guimaraes AC, Lima JC. The lipid profile and coronary artery disease. Arq Bras Cardiol 1994;63(2):101-6.

Oganov RG, et al. Increased risk of death from coronary heart disease in men with low blood concentration of total cholesterol and low density lipoprotein cholesterol according to data from a prospective epidemiologic study in Moscow and Leningrad within the framework of Soviet-American cooperation. Ter Arkh 1991;63(1):6-11.

Park Y, et al. Effect of conjugated linoleic acid on body composition in mice. Lipids 1997 Aug;32(8):853-8.

Sarchiapone M, et al. Further evidence for low serum cholesterol and suicidal behaviour. J Affect Disord 2000 Dec;61(1-2):69-71.

Singh TK. An assessment of serum lipid and lipoprotein levels in patients with ischaemic heart disease. Ann Acad Med Singapore 1992 Nov;21(6):773-80.

Starfield B. Is US health really the best in the world? JAMA 2000;284(4):483-5.

Thom E. Hydroxycitrate (HCA) in the treatment of obesity. Int J Obes Relat Metab Disord 1996;20 (Suppl 4):75.

Zureik M, et al. Decline in serum total cholesterol and the risk of death from cancer. Epidemiology 1997 Mar;8(2):137-43.

Chapter 6

Ahumada Hemer H, et al. Variations in serum lipids and lipoproteins throughout the menstrual cycle. Fertil Steril 1985 Jul;44(1):80-4.

Backstrom T, et al. The role of hormones and hormonal treatments in premenstrual syndrome. CNS Drugs 2003;17(5):325-42.

Barad D, et al. Update on the use of dehydroepiandrosterone supplementation among women with diminished ovarian function. J Assist Reprod Genet 2007 Dec;24(12):629-34.

Casson PR, et al. Dehydroepiandrosterone supplementation augments ovarian stimulation in poor responders: a case series. Hum Reprod 2000 Oct;15(10):2129-32.

Cwikel J. Psychological interactions with infertility among women. Eur J Obstet Gynecol Reprod Biol 2004 Dec 1;117(2):126-31.

Damti OB. Stress and distress in infertility among women. Harefuah 2008 Mar;147(3):256-60.

Moskowitz D. A comprehensive review of the safety and efficacy of bioidentical hormones for the management of menopause and related health risks. Altern Med Rev 2006 Sep;11(3):208-23.

Parker CR Jr, Mahesh VB. Interrelationship between excessive levels of circulating androgens in blood and ovulatory failure. J Reprod Med 1976 Aug;17(2):75-90.

Singh M. Progestins and neuroprotection: are all progestins created equal? Minerva Endocrinol 2007 Jun;32(2):95-102.

Sitruk-Ware R. New hormonal therapies and regimens in the postmenopause: routes of administration and timing of initiation. Climacteric 2007 Oct;10(5):358-70.

Smolarczyk R, et al. Lipid metabolism in women with threatened abortion. Ginekol Pol 1996 Oct;67(10):481-7.

Chapter 7

Bayne CW, et al. Serenoa repens (Permixon): a 5alpha-reductase types I and II inhibitor-new evidence in a coculture model of BPH. Prostate 1999 Sep 1;40(4):232-41.

Dzugan SA. Integrative management of erectile dysfunction. Life Extension 2005 Oct;77-82.

Habib FK, et al. Serenoa repens (Permixon) inhibits the 5alpha-reductase activity of human prostate cancer cell lines without interfering with PSA expression. Int J Cancer 2005 Mar 20;114(2):190-4.

Hryb DJ, et al. The effect of extracts of the roots of the stinging nettle (Urtica dioica) on the interaction of SHBG with its receptor on human prostatic membranes. Planta Med 1995 Feb;61(1):31-2.

Kandeel FR, et al. Male sexual function and its disorders: physiology, pathophysiology, clinical investigation, and treatment. Endocr Rev 2001 Jun;23(3):342-88.

Lunenfeld B. Aging men—challenges ahead. Asian J Androl 2001 Sep;3(3):161-8.

Lunenfeld B. Androgen therapy in the aging male. World J Urol 2003 Nov;21(5):292-305.

Nikoobakht M, Pourkasmaee M, Nasseh H. The relationship between lipid profile and erectile dysfunction. Urol J 2005 Winter;2(1):40-4.

Om As, Chung KW. Dietary zinc deficiency alters 5 alpha-reduction and aromatization of testosterone and androgen and estrogen receptors in rat liver. J Nutr 1996 Apr;126(4):842-88.

Schmidt M, Renner C, Loffler G. Progesterone inhibits glucocorticoid-dependent aromatase induction in human adipose fibroblasts. J Endocrinol 1998 Sep;158(3):401-7.

Schottner M, Gansser D, Spiteller G. Lignans from the roots of Urtica dioica and their metabolites bind to human sex hormone binding globulin (SHBG). Planta Med 1997 Dec;63(6):529-32.

Singh YN, Singh NN. Therapeutic potential of kava in the treatment of anxiety disorders. CNS Drugs 2002;16(11):731-43.

Slob AK, et al. Intracavernous injection during diagnostic screening for erectile dysfunction; five-year experience with over 600 patients. J Sex Marital Ther 2002 Jan;28(1):61-70.

Tilakaratne A, Soory M. Effects of the anti-androgen finasteride on 5 alpha-reduction of androgens in the presence of progesterone in human gingival fibroblasts; modulatory actions of the alkaline phosphatase inhibitor levamisole. J Periodontal Res 2000 Aug;35(4):179-85.

Vrentzos GE, et al. Dyslipidemia as a risk factor for erectile dysfunction. Curr Med Chem 2007;14(16):1765-70.

Wei M, et al. Total cholesterol and high density lipoprotein cholesterol as important predictors of erectile dysfunction. Am J Epidemiol 1994 Nov 15;140(10):930-7.

Werner, Michael A. MD, website: http://www.andropausespecialist.com

Chapter 8

Alvarez GG, Ayas NT. The impact of daily sleep duration on health: A review of the literature. Prog Cardiovasc Nurs 2004 Spring;19(2):56-9.

Baulieu EE, et al. Dehydroepiandrosterone (DHEA), DHEA sulfate, and aging: contribution of the DHEAge study to a sociobiomedical issue. Proc Natl Acad Sci USA 2000 Apr 11;97(8):4279-84.

Bellipanni G, et al. Effects of melatonin in perimenopausal and menopausal women: our personal experience. Ann NY Acad Sci 2005 Dec;1057:393-402.

Bouhnik Y, et al. Short-chain fructo-oligosaccharide administration dose-dependently increases fecal bifidobacteria in healthy humans. J Nutr 1999;129:113-6.

Brush MG et al. Pyridoxine in the treatment of premenstrual syndrome: a retrospective survey in 630 patients. Br J Clin Pract 1988 Nov;42(11):448-52.

Cajochen C, et al. Role of melatonin in the regulation of human circadian rhythms and sleep. J Neuroendocrinology 2003;15:432-37.

Claustrat B, et al. Melatonin secretion is supersensitivity to light in migraine. Cephalalgia 2004 Feb; 24(2): 128-33.

Clouatre DL. Kava kava; examining new reports of toxicity. Toxicol Lett 2004 Apr 15;150(1):85-96.

DeLeo V, et al. Assessment of the association of kava-kava extract and hormone replacement therapy in the treatment of postmenopause anxiety. Minerva Ginecol 2000 Jun;52(6):263-7.

Dzugan SA, Smith RA. The simultaneous restoration of neurohormonal and metabolic integrity as a very promising method of migraine management. Bull Urg Rec Med 2003;4:622-8.

Dzugan S. The Migraine Cure. 2006, Dragon Door Publications, Inc., USA

Ford ES, Mokdad AH. Dietary magnesium intake in a national sample of US adults. J Nutr 2003;133:2879-82.

Gagnier JJ. The therapeutic potential of melatonin in migraines and other headache types. Altern Med Rev 2001 Aug;6(4):383-9.

Head KA. Estriol: safety and efficacy. Altern Med Rev 1998 Apr;3(2):101-3.

Kirjavainen PV, et al. New aspects of probiotics—a novel approach in the management of food allergy. Allergy 1999;54:909-15.

Li W, et al. Sex steroid hormones exert biphastic effects on cytosolic magnesium ions in cerebral vascular smooth muscles cells: possible relationships to migraine frequency in premenstrual syndromes and stroke incidence. Brain Res Bull 2001 Jan 1;54(1):83-9.

Lu WZ, et al. Melatonin improves bowel symptoms in female patients with irritable bowel syndrome: a double-blind placebo-controlled study. Aliment Pharmacol Ther 2005 Nov 15;22(10):927-34.

Mauskop A, et al. Intravenous magnesium sulphate relieves migraine attacks in patients with low serum ionized magnesium levels: a pilot study. Clin Sci (Lond) 1994;89:633-6.

Mauskop A, et al. Serum ionized magnesium levels and serum ionized calcium/ionized magnesium ratios in women with menstrual migraine. Headache 2002 Apr;42(4):242-8.

Morales AJ, et al. Effects of replacement dose of dehydroepiandrosterone in men and women of advancing age. J Clin Endocrinol Metab 1994;78:1360-7.

Peres FP, et al. Melatonin, 3 mg, is effective for migraine prevention. Neurology 2004 Aug;63:757.

Pittler MH, Ernst E. Kava extract for treating anxiety. Cochrane Database Syst Rev 2002;(2):CD003383.

Pittler MH, Ernst E. Kava extract for treating anxiety. Cochrane Database Syst Rev 2003;(1):CD003383.

Saris NE, et al. Magnesium: an update on physiological, clinical, and analytical aspects. Clinica Chimica Acta 2000;294:1-26.

Suarez E. Relations of trait depression and anxiety to low lipid and lipoprotein concentrations in healthy young adult women. Psychosomatic Med May-June 1999;61(3):273-9.

Taubert K. Magnesium in migraine: Results of a multicenter pilot study. Fortschr Med 1994;112:328-30.

Walker AF, et al. Magnesium supplementation alleviates premenstrual symptoms of fluid retention. J Womens Health 1998 Nov;7(9):1157-65.

Chapter 9

Adler GK, et al. Neuroendocrine abnormalities in fibromyalgia. Curr Pain Headache Rep 2002 Aug;6(4):289-98.

Bennett RM. Fibromyalgia: the commonest cause of widespread pain. Compr Ther 1995 Jun;21(6):269-75.

Buyon JP, et al. The effect of combined estrogen and progesterone hormone replacement therapy on disease activity in SLE: A randomized trial. Ann Int Med 2005 Jun 21;142(12):part 1:953-62.

Chung N, et al. STATT: a titrate-to-goal study of simvastatin in Asian patients with coronary heart disease. Simvastatin Treats Asians to Target. Clin Ther 2001 Jun;23(6):858-70.

Citera G, et al. The effect of melatonin in patients with fibromyalgia: a pilot study. Clin Rheumatol 2000;19(1):9-13.

Dzugan S. Therapeutic options for fibromyalgia. Life Extension 2005 Jul;77-83

Gupta A, Silman AJ. Psychological stress and fibromyalgia: a review of the evidence suggesting a neuroendocrine link. Arthritis Res Ther 2004;6(3):98-106.

Lahita RG. Sex hormones and systemic lupus erythematosus. Rheum Dis Clin North Am 2000 Nov;26(4):956-68.

Matsumoto Y. Fibromyalgia syndrome. Nippon Rinsho 1999 Feb;57(2):364-9.

Nicolodi M, Sicuteri F. Fibromyalgia and migraine, two faces of the same mechanism. Serotonin as the common clue for pathogenesis and therapy. Adv Exp Med Biol 1996;398:373-9.

Petri M. Sex hormones and systemic lupus erythematosus. Lupus 2008;17(5):412-5.

Reiffenberger DH, Amundson LH. Fibromyalgia syndrome: a review. Am Fam Physician 1996 Apr;53(5):1698-712.

Rohr UD, Herold J. Melatonin deficiencies in women. Maturitas 2002 Apr 15;41 Suppl 1:S85-104.

Russo EG. Clinical endocannabinoid deficiency (CECD): can this concept explain therapeutic benefits of cannabis in migraine, fibromyalgia, irritable bowel syndrome and other treatment-resistant conditions? Neuro Endocrinol Lett 2004 Feb-Apr;25(1-2):31-9.

Sawalha AH, Kovats S. Dehydroepiandrosterone in systemic lupus erythematosus. Curr Rheumatol Rep 2008 Aug;10(4):286-91.

Schochat T, Beckmann C. Sociodemographic characteristics, risk factors and reproductive history in subjects with fibromyalgia—results of a population-based case-control study. Z Rheumatol 2003 Feb;62(1):46-59.

Thompson D, et al. Fibromyalgia: an overview. Curr Psychiatry Rep 2003 Jul;5(3):211-7.

Zandman-Goddard G, et al. Gender and autoimmunity. Autoimmun Rev 2007 Jun;6(6):366-72.

Chapter 10

Augustin AJ, et al. Cause and prevention of oxidative DHEA protects damage to the eye. Current knowledge. Ophthalmologe 2001 Aug;98(8):776-96.

DellaCroce JT, Vitale AT. Hypertension and the eye. Curr Opin Ophthalmol 2008 Nov;19(6):493-8.

Fraser-Bell S, et al. Cardiovascular risk factors and age-related macular degeneration: the Los Angeles Latino Eye Study. Am J Ophthalmol 2008 Feb;145(2):308-16.

Klein R, et al. Further observations on the association between smoking and the long-term incidence and progression of age-related macular degeneration: the Beaver Dam Eye Study. Arch Ophthalmol 2008 Jan;126(1):115-21.

Li C, et al. Distribution and composition of esterified and unesterified cholesterol in extra-macular drusen. Exp Eye Res 2007 Aug;85(2):192-201. Epub 2007 Apr 19.

Lundmark PO, et al. Role of melatonin in the eye and ocular dysfunctions. Vis Neurosci 2006 Nov-Dec;23(6):853-62.

Malek G, et al. Apolipoprotein B in cholesterol-containing drusen and basal deposits of human eyes with age-related maculopathy. Am J Patholog Sci 2003 Feb;162(2):413-25.

Richer S, et al. Double-masked, placebo-controlled, randomized trial of lutein and antioxidant supplementation in the intervention of atrophic age-related macular degeneration: the Veterans LAST study (Lutein Antioxidant Supplementation Trial). Optometry 2004 Apr;75(4):216-30.

Schutt F, et al. Vitamins and trace elements in age-related macular degeneration. Current recommendations, based on the results of the AREDS study. Ophthalmologe 2002 Apr;99(4):301-3.

Tamer C, Oksuz H, Sogut S. Serum dehydroepiandrosterone sulphate level in age-related macular degeneration. Am J Ophthalmol 2007 Feb;143(2):212-6.

Tan JS, et al. Dietary antioxidants and the long-term incidence of age-related macular degeneration: the Blue Mountains Eye Study. Ophthalmology 2008 Feb;115(2):334-41.

Yi C, et al. Effects of melatonin in age-related macular degeneration. Ann NY Acad Sci 2005 Dec;1057:384-92.

Yost D. Preventing Macular Degeneration A New Theory. Life Extension 2008 Dec;36-43.

Zarbin ME. Current concepts in the pathogenesis of age-related macular degeneration. Arch Ophthalmol 2004;122:598-614.

Chapter 11

Akin LK. Pediatric and adolescent bipolar disorder: medical resources. Med Ref Serv Q 2001 Fall;20(3):31-44.

Atmaca M, et al. Serum leptin and cholesterol levels in patients with bipolar disorder. Neuropsychbiology 2002;46(4):176-9.

Bernstein BE. Anxiety disorder: social phobia and selective mutism. July 6, 2005. Available at: http://www.emedicine.com/ped/topic2660.htm. Accessed February 10, 2009.

Biederman J, et al. Family-environment risk factors for attention-deficit hyperactivity disorder. A test of Rutter's indicators of adversity. Arch Gen Psychiatry 1995 Jun;52(6):464-70.

Boston PF, et al. Cholesterol and mental disorder. Br J Psychiatry 1996 Dec;169(6):682-9.

Brunner J, et al. [Cholesterol, omega-3 fatty acids, and suicide risk: empirical evidence and pathophysiological hypotheses][Article in German] Fortschr Neurol Psychiatr 2001 Oct;69(10):460-7.

Cassidy F, Carroll BJ. Hypocholesterolemia during mixed manic episodes. Eur Arch Psychiatry Clin Neurosci 2002 Jun; 252(3):110-14.

Chavira DA, et al. Comorbidity of generalized social anxiety disorder and depression in a pediatric primary care sample J Affect Disord 2004 Jun;80(2-3):163-71.

Dulcan M. Practice parameters for the assessment and treatment of children, adolescents, and adults with attention-deficit/ hyperactivity disorder. Am Acad Child Adolesc Psychiatry 1997 Oct; 36(10 Suppl): 85S-121S.

Dzugan S. A new therapeutic option for behavioral disorders. Life Extension 2006 Feb;71-4.

Ellison LF, Morrison HI. Low serum cholesterol concentration and risk of suicide. Epidemiology 2001 Mar;12(2):168-72.

Faraone SV, Biederman J. Neurobiology of attention-deficit hyperactivity disorder. Biol Psychiatry 1998 Nov 15;44(10): 951-8.

Girardi NL, et al. Blunted catecholamine responses after glucose ingestion in children with attention deficit disorder. Pediatr Res 1995 Oct;38(4):539-42.

Glueck CJ, et al. Hypocholesterolemia and affective disorders. Am J Med Sci 1994 Oct;308(4):218-25.

Goldman LS, et al. Diagnosis and treatment of attention-deficit/ hyperactivity disorder in children and adolescents. Council on Scientific Affairs, American Medical Association. JAMA 1998 Apr 8;279(14):1100-7.

Golomb BA, Stattin H, Mednick S. Low cholesterol and violent crime. J Psychiatr Res 2000 Jul-Oct;34(4-5):301-9.

Hawthon K, et al. Low serum cholesterol and suicide. Br J Psychiatry 1993 Jun;162:818-25.

Mercugliano M. What is attention-deficit/hyperactivity disorder? Pediatr Clin N Am 1999 Oct;46(5):831-43.

Poulton A, Cowell CT. Slowing of growth in height and weight on stimulants: a characteristic pattern. J Paediatr Child Health 2003 Apr;39(3):180-5.

Rabe-Jablonska J, Poprawska I. Levels of serum total cholesterol and LDL-cholesterol in patients with major depression in acute period and remission. Med Sci Monit 2000 May-Jun;6(3):539-47.

Rao JK, et al. Response to growth hormone in attention deficit hyperactivity disorder: effects of methylphenidate and pemoline therapy. Pediatrics 1998 Aug;102 (2Pt 3):497-500.

Robison LM, et al. Is attention deficit hyperactivity disorder increasing among girls in the US? Trends in diagnosis and the prescribing of stimulants. CNS Drugs 2002;16(2):129-37.

Rohde LA, et al. ADHD in a school sample of Brazilian adolescents: a study of prevalence, comorbid conditions, and impairments. J Am Acad Child Adolesc Psychiatry 1999 Jun;38(6):716-22.

Rohde LA, Halpern R. Recent advances on attention deficit/hyperactivity disorder. J Pediatr (Rio J) 2004 Apr;80(2 Suppl):S61-70.

Safer DJ, et al. Increased methylphenidate usage for attention deficit disorder in the 1990s. Pediatrics 1995 Dec;98(6 Pt 1): 1084-8.

Safer DJ, et al. Concomitant psychotropic medication for youths. Am J Psychiatry 2003 Mar;160(3):438-49.

Spivak B, et al. Circulatory levels of catecholamines, serotonin and lipids in attention deficit hyperactivity disorder. Acta Psychiatr Scand 1999 Apr;99(4):300-4.

Steegmans PH, et al. Higher prevalence of depressive symptoms in middle-aged men with low serum cholesterol levels. Psychosom Med 2000 Mar-Apr;62(2):205-11.

Strous RD, et al. Analysis of neurosteroid levels in attention deficit hyperactivity disorder. Int J Neuropsychopharmacol 2001 Sep;4(3):259-64.

Tannock R. Attention deficit hyperactivity disorder: advances in cognitive, neurobiological, and genetic research. J Child Psychol Psychiatry 1998 Jan;39(1):65-99.

Chapter 12

Adams WJ, Morris DL. Short-course cimetidine and survival with colorectal cancer. Lancet 1994 Dec 24;344(9039-3940):1768-9.

Altshuler LL, et al. Treatment of Depression in Women 2001: Expert Consensus Guideline Series. Postgraduate Medicine, March 2001. New York: McGraw Hill, 2001.

Apter SJ, Eriksson CJ. The role of social isolation in the effects of alcohol on corticosterone and testosterone levels of alcohol-preferring and non-preferring rats. Alcohol Alcohol 2006 Jan-Feb;41(1):33-8.

Augustynska B, et al. Menstrual cycle in women addicted to alcohol during the first week following drinking cessation—changes of sex hormones levels in relation to selected clinical features. Alcohol Alcohol 2007 Mar-Apr;42(2):80-3.

Bergman B, Brismar B. Hormone levels and personality traits in abusive and suicidal male alcoholics. Alcohol Clin Exp Res 1994 Apr;18(2):311-6.

Buydens-Branchey L, Branchey M. Association between low plasma levels of cholesterol and relapse in cocaine addicts. Psychosomatic Med 2003;65:86-91.

Coiro V, et al. Adrenocorticotropic hormone/cortisol response to physical exercise in abstinent alcoholic patients. Alcohol Clin Exp Res 2007 May;31(5):901-6.

Dai X, et al. Response of the HPA-axis to alcohol and stress as a function of alcohol dependence and family history of alcoholism. Psychoneuroendocrinology 2007 Apr;32(3):293-305.

Dzugan SA, Smith RA, Kuznetsov AS. Five years survivorship in bilateral lung cancer. Non-surgical treatment with palliative radiotherapy and bioimmunotherapy. Health Don. 2006;1:38-42.

Dzugan S. Natural strategies for managing insomnia. Life Extension 2006 Dec;77-80.

Dzugan SA, Rozakis GW, Smith RA. The role of hormonorestorative therapy in treatment of major illnesses. In: 15th Annual World Congress on Anti-Aging Medicine and Regenerative Biomedical Technologies. Las Vegas, NV, USA; 2007:156-8.

Endogenous Hormones and Prostate Cancer Collaborative Group, et al. Endogenous sex hormones and prostate cancer: A collaborative analysis of 18 prospective studies. J Natl Cancer Inst 2008 Feb 6;100(3):170-83. Epub 2008 Jan 29.

Fairchild G, et al. Cortisol diurnal rhythm and stress reactivity in male adolescents with early-onset or adolescence-onset conduct disorder. Biol Psychiatry 2008 Oct 1;64(7):599-606.

Glueck CJ, et al. Hypocholesterolemia, hypertriglyceridemia, suicide, and suicide ideation in children hospitalized for psychiatric diseases. Pediatr Res 1994 May;35(5):602-10.

Haines C. Cimetidine: Common heartburn remedy complements conventional cancer therapy. Life Extension 2007 May.

Heinz A, et al. severity of depression in abstinent alcoholics is associated with monoamine metabolites and dehydroepiandrosterone-sulfate concentrations. Psychiatry Res 1999 Dec 20;89(2):97-106.

Ho WK, et al. Comparison of plasma hormonal levels between heroin-addicted and normal subjects. Clin Chim Acta 1977 Mar 15;75(3):415-9.

Iribarren C, et al. Serum total cholesterol and mortality. Confounding factors and risk modification in Japanese-American men. JAMA 1995 Jun 28;273(24):1926-32.

Jensvold MF, et al. Psychopharmacology and women: Sex, gender and hormones. Washington DC: American Psychiatric Press, 1996.

Kessler RC, et al. Prevalence, severity, and comorbidity of twelve-month DSM-IV disorders in the National Comorbidity Survey Replication (NCS-R). Archives Gen Psychiatry 2005 Jun;62(6):617-27.

Lefranc F, et al. Cimetidine, an unexpected anti-tumor agent, and its potential for the treatment of glioglastoma. Int J Oncol 2006 May;28(5):1021-30.

Leibenluft E, ed. Gender Differences in Mood and Anxiety: Review of Psychiatry, vol. 18. Washington, DC: American Psychiatric Press, 1999.

Maccari S, et al. Plasma cholesterol and triglycerides in heroin addicts. Drug Alcohol Depend 1991 Dec 31;29(2):183-7.

Maneesh M, et al. Alcohol abuse-duration dependent decrease in plasma testosterone and antioxidants in males. Indian J Physiol Pharmacol 2006 Jul-Sep;50(3):291-6.

Markopoulou K, et al. The ratio of cortisol/DHEA in treatment resistant depression. Psychoneuroendocrinology 2009 Jan;34(1):19-26.

Marks LS, et al. Effect of testosterone replacement therapy on prostate tissue in men with late-onset hypogonadism: a randomized controlled trial. JAMA 2006;296:2351-61.

Morrow AL, et al. Hypothalamic-pituitary-adrenal axis modulation of GABAergic neuroactive steroids influences ethanol sensitivity and drinking behavior. Dialogues Clin Neurosci 2006;8(4):463-77.

Olive MF, et al. Stimulation of endorphin neurotransmission in the nucleus accumbens by ethanol, cocaine, and amphetamine. J Neurosci 2001 Dec 1;21(23):RC184.

Schmidt PJ, et al. Estrogen replacement in perimenopausal-related depression: a preliminary report. Am J Obstet Gynecol 2000;183:414-20.

Smith RA, Dzugan SA. Survival indicates immune restoration is an effective treatment in extensive lung cancer. In: Fourth scientific conference of Anti-Aging medicine. Las-Vegas, USA; 1996:26-7.

Smith RA, Dzugan SA et al. Covariance of natural killer cells elevation with extended survival during neuroimmunotherapy with subcutaneous low-dose IL-2 and the pineal immunomodulating neurohormone melatonin. Bull Urg Rec Med 2001;2:20-3.

Smith RA, Dzugan SA. Role of immunorestorative therapy in Non Small-Cell Lung Cancer. In: 11th International Congress on Anti-Aging & Biomedical Technologies. Las Vegas, NV, USA; 2003:109-123.

Soares CN, et al. Efficacy of estadiol for the treatment of depressive disorders in perimenopausal women: a double-blind, randomized, placebo-controlled trial. Arch Gen Psychiatry 2001 Jun;58(6):529-34.

Stewart DE, et al. Depression, estrogen and the Women's Health Initiative. Psychosomatics 2004 Oct;45:445-7.

Tadic SD, et al. Hypogonadism precedes liver feminization in chronic alcohol-fed male rats. Hepatology 2000 May;31(5):1135-40.

Tonnesen H, et al. Effect of cimetidine on survival after gastric cancer. Lancet 1988 Oct 29;2(8618):990-2.

Wilczek H, et al. Serum lipids in drug addicts. Vnitr Lek 2004 Aug;50(8):584-6.

http://www.cdc.gov/Alcohol/quickstats/underage_drinking.htm

Yoshimatsu K, et al. Can the survival of patients with recurrent disease after curative resection of colorectal cancer be prolonged by the administration of cimetidine? Gan To Kagaku Ryoho 2006 Nov;33(12): 1730-2.

Zalewska-Kaszubska J, et al. Lack of changes in beta-endorphin plasma levels after repeated treatment with fluoxetine: possible implications for the treatment of alcoholism, pilot study. Pharmazie 2008 Apr;63(4):308-11.

Image Sources

- Unhappy young couple in bedroom: © Marin Conic

- Femme sommeil: © guillaume

- Free from Alcholism: © Mikhail Tolstoy

- Thoughtful Old Man: © NiDerLander

- A woman is praying to god with hope: © memo

- Woman holds hand on pain neck: © Tatyana Gladskih

- Woman Scared: © Tatyana Gladskih

- Migraine headache: © Laurin Rinder

- Breast cancer pink ribbon: © C Claudia

- Digestive System: © OOZ

- Wrist injury: © Sielemann

- Love: © Franz Pfluegl

- Couple in living room with baby smiling: © Monkey Business

- vintage scales showing imbalance: © James Steidl

All images from fotolia.com

Index

 **Sergey A. Dzugan, MD, PhD** is co-founder of the Dzugan Institute of Restorative Medicine. Dr. Dzugan graduated from the Donetsk State Medical Institute (Ukraine) with a Doctorate of Medicine in 1979. After medical school, he performed his residency in general and cardiovascular surgery and became the Head of Heart Services in 1985. Dr. Dzugan has had special training in vascular surgery, combustiology, microsurgery, arrhythmology, heart surgery, genetic testing, pedagogics and psychology. Dr. Dzugan was a distinguished and highly trained educator, physician, and surgeon in the Ukraine.

In 1990, he received his PhD in Medical Science concerning heart rhythm disorder, and subsequently became Assistant Professor at the Donetsk State Medical Institute. In May of 1991, he became the first Chief of the Department of Cardiovascular Surgery and Senior Heart Surgeon, in Donetsk District Regional Hospital, Ukraine.

In March of 1993, he became Associate Professor at Donetsk State Medical University. Dr. Dzugan performed a wide spectrum of operations for children and adults, including congenital and acquired heart diseases, and rhythm disorders. As the Head of Heart Surgery, he had the highest medical skills and qualifications which can be awarded in his former country. As a practicing physician, Dr. Dzugan always found himself more in favor of holistic and natural medicines rather than synthetic. He always believed that strengthening one's immune system would do more to improve health than treating problems after they occur. Because of this, while performing heart surgeries, Dr. Dzugan became more interested in the preventive aspects of heart disease and began studying hormone treatments.

Dr. Dzugan moved to the United States from Ukraine in 1995, and in 1996 became a scientific consultant to Dr. Arnold Smith at the North

282 - The Dzugan Principle: Your Blood Doesn't Lie

Central Mississippi Regional Center in Greenwood, Mississippi. His role there was to stay current on the latest advances in nutriceutical treatments with a particular focus on ways to improve immunity, and the ability of patients to fight cancer. Dr. Dzugan worked with the Cancer Center for more than 7 years and was a principle consultant of Anti-Aging strategy and biological therapy of cancer. The Cancer Center was active in clinical research, and Dr. Dzugan's scholarly background as a clinical researcher helped proceed in a more organized and scientific fashion. In 1998, he has become board certified by the American Academy of Anti-Aging Medicine. His employer at the North Central Mississippi Regional Cancer Center has expressed stated that "Dr. Dzugan is extremely valuable to patient care and his role differentiates the North Central Mississippi Regional Cancer Center from that of any other centers in the States, because no other center has a full time well qualified staff person to meet the same function." Dr. Smith believes that "Dr. Dzugan is a brilliant, gifted physician whose talents, we believe, would make a significant contribution to the nation."

In 2001, Dr. Dzugan suggested a new hypothesis of hypercholesterolemia and developed a new statin-free method of high cholesterol treatment. He also developed a unique multimodal program for migraine management.

In October 2003, he moved to Ft. Lauderdale, Florida, and became the Manager of the Advisory Department at the Life Extension Foundation. Later, he became President of Life Extension Scientific Information Inc.

In August 2006, Dr. Dzugan left the Life Extension Foundation to create The Migraine Program, a scientific organization that consults with physicians to develop the optimal plans for their patients to prevent migraine.

Dr. Dzugan was accepted (June, 30 2006) to the International Academy of Creative Endeavors (Moscow, Russia) as a Corresponding Member of the Academy for the outstanding contribution to the development of new methods of hypercholesterolemia and migraine treatment. In December 2007, Dr. Dzugan was awarded with an Honoree Medal by this Academy, for his personal input into the acquisition of science, culture, physical betterment of the nation, and strengthening of friendship between nations. He performed presentations multiple times at the prestigious International Congress on Anti-Aging Medicine. The topics of his presentations were "Hypercholesterolemia Treatment: a New Hypothesis or Just an Accident?", "Role of Immunorestorative Therapy in Non Small-Cell Lung Cancer", "A New Method of Migraine Treatment: The Simultaneous Restoration of Neurohormonal and Metabolic Integrity", "Hypercholesterolemia Treatment: a New Statin Free Method", "The Effect of Multimodal Treatment Program in Migraine Management", "The Role of Hormonorestorative Therapy in Hypercholesterolemia Treatment", and "The Role of Hormonorestorative Therapy in the Treatment of Major Illnesses".He also was a speaker at the Third Annual Mississippi Partnership for Cancer Control in Underserved Populations Conference. The workshop was titled "Ask the Expert: Questions on Lung Cancer."

Dr. Dzugan is the author of 134 publications in medical journals, and these publications include surgical, oncological, academic and anti-aging topics. Also, several articles were published in Life Extension Magazine and The South African Journal of Natural Medicine. He is the author of "The Migraine Cure" book, and holder of 3 patents (all related to heart surgery). Dr. Dzugan is a member of the Medical Advisory Board at Life Extension Magazine.

Dr. Dzugan's current primary interests are physiologic therapy for elevated cholesterol, migraine, fatigue, fibromyalgia, behavioral and hormonal disorders.

George Rozakis, MD, is co-founder of the Dzugan Institute of Restorative Medicine. Dr. Rozakis is a pioneering Lasik eye surgeon who has received global awards and patents for his contribution to laser surgery. He continues to develop groundbreaking technologies using implantable contact lenses, which ends patients' need for glasses. Dr. Rozakis graduated with a degree in biomedical engineering from Case Western Reserve University, studied medicine at Cornell Medical College, and studied ophthalmology at the Duke University Eye Center.

In 2004, he became interested in the field of anti-aging medicine while he was on vacation and met a doctor who was implementing this type of care to his patients. Encouraged by what he heard, he attended a conference in Chicago on Anti-Aging Medicine and found it to be a highly fragmented area without clear direction. Sensing that this was similar to the early days of Lasik, Dr. Rozakis decided to return to these conferences and identify the most knowledgable thinker in the field of Anti-Aging Medicine. Serendipitously, this led to his meeting Dr. Sergey Dzugan, M.D., Ph.D.

Dr. Dzugan trained Dr. Rozakis in anti-aging medicine and assisted him in delivering it to many of his Lasik patients who subsequently experienced a profound improvement in their appearance, quality of life, and illnesses. Over the course of two years, it became completely clear to Dr. Rozakis that this treatment approach, which involved use of vitamins, supplements, and bioidentical hormones, held great promise in reversing the symptoms of aging and combatting many diseases that afflict patients over the age of 40, as well as illnesses in younger patients such as ADHD, alcoholism, and migraine.

Dr. Rozakis developed the Macular Program to use anti-aging medicine to slow or stop the progression of macular degeneration. As he and Dr. Dzugan predicted, recent studies in the *American Journal of Ophthalmology* have shown that patients who develop macular degeneration have profoundly subnormal levels of hormones. Dr. Dzugan and Dr. Rozakis are developing strategies to reverse these deficiencies, in the attempt to halt this devastating cause of blindness. Ophthalmology, they discovered, is an important contact point for Restorative Medicine, not only for patients who need reading glasses, but even for those with glaucoma and diabetic eye disease. This realization has taken Dr. Rozakis full circle back to his specialty with an exciting message that will preserve vision for millions.

Dr. Rozakis is the author of 2 textbooks, more than 30 publications in medical journals, and 4 inventions in ophthalmology.

Contacting the Authors:

If you would like to learn more about the authors or order additional books, please visit:

www.yourblooddoesntlie.com

For Physicians:

If you would like to learn more about the Dzugan Principle, bioidentical hormones and restorative medicine, please visit:

www.yourblooddoesntlie.com

and click "I am a Physician"